A Rebel's Take On Depression

BREAKDOWN

Eleanor O'Rourke

This book is for you...
I hope it helps.
Hang in there.
The light does come back.

ONE

The Fall

"The world breaks everyone, and afterward,
some are strong at the broken places"

—ERNEST HEMINGWAY

I looked at the clock on the wall. Another hour gone, and still no words on the computer screen. This time it was serious.

For as long as I can remember, I've been able to write. Until one day, when the words just stopped coming. I couldn't blame it on stress or tiredness. I wasn't busy and I wasn't procrastinating.

Something happened... and I lost my mind.

It's difficult to write without a mind, though the state of "No mind" or "Zen mind" seems quite popular at the moment. "Mindfulness" is a bit of a strange term as it implies a mind that's full, which of course is the last thing you want when searching for inner peace.

My mind got so full that it cracked open.

Leonard Cohen once famously wrote "there's a crack in everything – that's where the light gets in." What he omitted to mention was that this crack also provides the means by which the dark can emerge from its psychic depths. It erupts like black volcanic lava seeking release, paralyzing its victims as they attempt to flee.

This is what happened...

The relationship with my boyfriend had ended three months previously, although in MY mind it hadn't really ended. It's just that all the energy had gone out of the relationship. This meant for him, it was over. It meant for me that the relationship was on hold until I could figure out a master plan to get the energy back, after which, everything would be wonderful and just like it was at the beginning.

Part of this master plan meant "giving him space." It was the emotionally mature option. After all men find commitment difficult and highly creative men are hard wired to seek out diversion and new things. Being a creativity coach, I know a lot about creativity. It is our natural state, before we become civilized. As children, we are in a constant state of exploration. A blue plastic truck is a source of delight, until we hold it, taste it, and see what it's capable of. Then we discard it because we've just found a yellow duck, or a bag of carrots.

It stands to reason that the same principle applies to people. We would be slightly alarmed by a child that plays happily with the blue truck for say five years. Lack of curiosity makes dull people and we like curious, creative boyfriends. Therefore we are ok for them to go walkabout from time to time. AS LONG AS THEY COME BACK.

He didn't come back.

This, like all unwelcome behaviour, is easily explained away by the independent woman. Out of sight, out of mind. He's busy with

STUFF. If he saw me again, he would remember how much he loved that blue truck. He would remember that it really was his favorite toy of all time and that he never wanted to be parted from it again.

All it would take, would be for us to meet.

In the meantime I gave him space. Three months of space. And then the perfect opportunity arose.

In romantic comedy, there is a term for this. It's called "the meet cute". If you are keen to write in this genre, it is important that your "meet cute" is not too contrived. The need to pick up the shoes you left under the bed is a bit lame. "Accidentally" running into him on the way to work, leaves no opportunity for plot development. A crowded commuter train doesn't lend itself to the passionate embrace required by Scene Two.

As fortune would have it, I was invited to a Music Industry awards dinner, a mere five minutes walk from his apartment. The time was right (evening). I would have a legitimate excuse to be dressed to the nines (not contrived at all!) so I sent a message. Breezy. Going here, would be lovely to see you, how about I pop in... that sort of thing.

The reality of course was not so breezy as it involved a considerable amount of pre-meet grooming, decisions about what to wear, decisions about what to wear underneath what to wear.

On the day I was so excited I could barely stay in my body. It was winter, and I pulled a hat down over my eyes in case the icy wind caused my mascara-rimmed eyes to water and streak. I rang the bell, so strange and so familiar at the same time, my heart was racing. I checked myself in the mirror of the lift, wondering how he was feeling – Curiosity? Was I new again?

He opened the door.

He was on the phone.

"Hi" his eyes kind of said, before gesturing me into the apartment. He carried on talking. It wasn't the "meet cute" I'd envisaged. I walked across the familiar/not familiar room, wondering whether to stand and look out of the window or sit down and look at the wall. I had no stage directions for this scenario. By now we should at least be wrapped in a warm embrace.

He glanced in my direction rotating one hand to signify that the other person was going on unnecessarily. I couldn't help thinking there were more effective ways of bringing the conversation to an end, like perhaps saying CAN I CALL YOU BACK? Then I remembered I was an emotionally mature woman so smiled and rolled my eyes as if to say "I know right, this stuff just happens. I'm totally cool and besides, I am now completely absorbed by some random thing going on outside the window."

The phone call ended and he greeted me in that friendly, sincere, practiced way. Like a politician who wanted to know if he could count on my vote. We chatted. Things became more familiar. Not strange any more.

We had always been able to talk. That was the best part. We found the same things absurd, tragic or hilarious. We were King and Queen of our own reality show. United in our narcissistic bubble, we made fun of convention, ridiculed the bland, and decapitated the boring with our razor sharp wit. I was just settling in for the opening credits of the sequel – The Return of the Queen – when he announced he had to be somewhere, so... lovely to see me and all that, but he had to get on, jump in the shower.

The brief thought flashed through my mind that whereas I had been through a lengthy procedure involving most of the bottles on my bathroom shelf (even the very expensive "'too special to use" gift ones) he hadn't given this "meet cute" very much consideration at all.

But I'm the opposite of needy, so I batted this unhelpful thought away. He was a busy man with important things that demanded his attention. I had an awards ceremony to get to, so also busy (mental note THIS IS NOT A COMPETITION).

I headed for the door – the place where our second date (the one in which we are BOTH NOT BUSY) would be established. The place where we would kiss and rekindle our passion, thus initiating an exchange of hilarious and hot text messages.

There was no kiss.

There was no second date.

I walked slowly to the venue. Partly because I was early and partly because I have never been able to walk in high heels. I run most places. I travel on an underground system that has gridded escalators. So I wear boots or trainers. I only wear heels when I can pull them from a carrier bag at the last minute.

But of course this would spoil the entrance.

An entrance that went completely unnoticed.

He didn't actually SAY it was a client meeting. Perhaps he was going on a date. With a really hot woman. One he was excited to see. One he wanted to jump in the shower for. Does anyone actually jump in a shower?

"Practice an attitude of gratitude." That's what the mindfulness people would tell you in a situation like this.

And I was grateful.

I was grateful that the pain in my feet took my attention away from the pain in my heart. I had to push the feelings down. Disappointment. Jealousy. Sadness. Push them down towards my toes. Bad feelings. Get back down there!

I arrived at the awards ceremony. There was bustle, clinking glasses, laughter, old faces I hadn't seen for 20 years. I looked great (inadvertently) and allowed myself a small feeling of superiority.

(Apparently 20 years in the hard drinking, druggy late nights of rock and roll can really age people. Who'd have guessed?!) But as the evening progressed, I felt more and more lonely.

Parties invoke a special kind of loneliness. I suppose that's where the word *alienation* comes from. The feeling of being an alien on a planet that has strange social customs – alcohol infused banter, sideways glances, endless small talk.

We used to do Big Talk. In the bath at the end of the day. Limbs curled around each other. Not listening to the low hum of the radio in the background, too wrapped up in each other's words. Interesting words. Animated conversations. In sharp contrast to...

I looked around the table. I could have made this into something funny. If I had someone to text. Someone who would really get it. Who would really get me.

No-one would ever really get me the way he did.

No-one.

Ever again.

Stop it! That's not helpful. Be here now. Mindfulness. Be engaged. I looked at the man on the opposite side of the table. It was difficult to imagine how I'd had such a major crush on him 20 years ago. He had numerous girlfriends of course, because the music business was like a huge magnet to attractive women. They arrived each evening, a giggling horde in skin-tight trousers and blow dried hair.

I was a working girl. That's how I survived the rock and roll circus. If you get a skill and you work really hard, then you don't have to be the lady in a bikini who gets sawn in half! You get to play in the game with the big boys. But you don't get to have an actual boyfriend.

On farms, in the lambing season, if a baby lamb dies, the farmer cuts its skin off and wraps it around an orphan that needs feeding.

The mother sheep is suspicious for a little while but it smells like her lamb so she accepts it as her own. After that the little waistcoat can be removed.

I got accepted into the boy's club.

But deep down I knew I was a fraud.

It was a great life. There was drama, creativity, spontaneity. The crew of a rock and roll tour didn't shuffle into an office at 9am, grey faced, bored, briefcase in one hand, latte in the other. They ARRIVED... in a venue that resembled an empty aircraft hangar, looking like the astronauts in *The Right Stuff*. They strode around, sniffed the air, lit up a Marlboro and said something along the lines of "Let's do this shit."

I know right? What's not to love? And I was in love... with a succession of these demi Gods. None of whom noticed me "in that way".

The women they loved were Goddesses, confident in their sexuality and their female power. The after show hook up was a bit like watching Greek mythology unfold, which of course turned quickly to tragedy, once the Goddesses realized their partners were on the prowl for fresh nymphs. Then all that wondrous power of theirs drained away. They became anxious, needy, and jealous.

When this happened I remembered how great it was being me. I wasn't anxious, needy or jealous! ON THE OUTSIDE. But of course under that false skin there was a different story going on.

Generally it was great to be me during the day but not so great during the night. Luckily on a rock and roll tour the nights are short. This was a time before Human Resources were invented, so working hours were very, very long.

Eventually, one of these demi Gods (who I had a six month crush on) did notice me. (Hurrah!) At a Thin Lizzy gig in Leicester. It was a two night show so no load out to do (Serendipity!) The crew were staying in a hotel, not a tour bus. (Bliss!)

We slept together.

I was giddy with the magical alchemy of what happens when feelings are FINALLY reciprocated, so spent most of the time hovering in an out of body experience thinking "Oh my God this is actually happening!" He turned to me afterwards, looked me in the eyes, and said those immortal words...

"You do know this doesn't mean anything don't you? It's not like we're an item or anything."

I laughed in what I hoped was a "well duh! OBVIOUSLY" kind of way. But I couldn't actually speak because I was busy pushing my feelings down. Rolling them up like a recently vacated sleeping bag, squishing the air out, pushing them as far down as possible. It takes effort and focus, but it's an essential skill for a pioneer, an independent woman in a man's world.

I looked across the table at him now. Bloated with alcohol, boring the woman sitting next to him.

He had no idea who I was.

Robbie Williams was on stage, saying something incomprehensible. A speech? A story? A segue?

Grateful.

Blessed.

Hashtag.

The last award was presented and I left before the long goodbyes and the long queue for the cloakroom. I couldn't afford a cab and needed to get the last train home. I was suddenly aware of the shoes again. If it hadn't been so cold I'd have taken them off and run to the station in stockinged feet.

I walked slowly, aware of a strange sensation in the pit of my stomach. Something was unfurling.

I got to the station and sat on a bench, waiting for the train. The wind hit my face. But I didn't care any more about the mascara.

I wanted to call him. I could have been there in five minutes. But somewhere inside, I knew that his date was over and by now they were both in bed, or in the bath, talking, laughing, amazed at how much they had in common. How new and exciting and filled with possibility everything was.

I finally accepted that our relationship had ended.

It was over.

I got on the train, desperate for the warmth that slowly seeped into my body. The sensation in my stomach had moved to my chest. This is what heartbreak feels like. A crack in the heart. But no light was coming in.

And then I realized what was happening. All those feelings that I'd shoved down. Years of them. They found a fault line.

Not loveable.
Not chosen.
Not the one.
Not the girlfriend.
Not good enough.
Not pretty enough.
Not clever enough.
Not funny enough.
Not.
Knot.
Unravelling.

I looked at my reflection in the train window and noticed the lines of mascara running down my face. Like rivers of molten black lava flowing from my heart of darkness.

All the judgments I'd had on other women – their pathetic neediness, their childish dependency, their clingy jealousy.

I was all of them.

He was right to end it. He had peeked under the sheep skin waistcoat and realized I was an imposter. He had discovered I wasn't the person I'd pretended to be.

But who was I?

I wanted someone to mother me; to hold me and say that everything was going to be alright; to tell me who I was.

Who I *really* was.

And then everything went dark.

TWO

May the Force Be with You

Depression is a strange beast, like a mythological creature with super-powers. I'm a fighter, but I prefer to fight against things I can see, and things I can describe with words. In general we call this "the real world".

But there's another world. One that's made of energy. A world we can't see and struggle to describe. In the past this energy world was the domain of madmen and religious fanatics. The mad could see and hear things that weren't part of the real world, so we locked them up in lunatic asylums. The religious fanatics could also see and hear things (visions of angels and the voice of God), but we had more respect for their experience, and turned them into saints.

Sometimes.

Obviously being a man helped in this scenario – Joan of Arc had to be burnt at the stake first, before being turned into a saint. It's all a bit arbitrary at the interface between the real world and the energy one.

Creative people venture in and out of the energy world, tuning in to the voice of intuition and the flash of imagination. If they're successful, we give them adulation and lots of money. If they're not, we could unknowingly walk past them, sleeping rough in shop doorways, and give them loose change. Success is of course entirely subjective. Tracy Emin's unmade bed, surrounded by used condoms, dirty underwear and empty vodka bottles sold for $3.5 million. One person's squalor is another person's high art.

"Ah but Tracy's bed wasn't just a bed", critics say, "it was an homage to heartbreak and depression. It was the essence of what she captured upon waking up from an alcohol fuelled binge." The depression and heartbreak of homeless people doesn't count of course, because they're less articulate at describing their condition.

Love exists in the energy world. The force of it can make us self-less, heroic or completely crazy. Descriptions of it can include romantic, sentimental, passionate, innocent, destructive, divine... yet it's one word – love. One inadequate word.

Depression exists in the energy world. Again, one word covers a multitude of states from feeling a bit disappointed to having the urge to jump off a bridge. I didn't have a lot of sympathy for people who were depressed, because I presumed they just weren't trying hard enough.

And then it happened to me. I fell into a dark place, where there seemed to be no energy at all. No desire to do anything. Meanwhile, above my head, there was an awful lot of energy holding me down. I was in a prison, but I was also my own prison guard, which made escape slightly complicated.

The medical world struggles to understand depression, but for me it was simple. Depression feels like a complete inability to manage energy.

Energy itself is a tricky word. We don't know exactly what it is, we just know how it feels – animation inside the body that becomes an impulse. Directed outwards, it can be used creatively. Directed inwards, it can become destructive.

It affects us in a variety of ways. Physically – we want to do things, but lack the energy to do them. Mentally – we want to do things but the energy is too chaotic, making us stressed or anxious. Emotionally – we want to do things but can't stop crying. Spiritually – we DON'T want to do things, because life feels random and pointless. Being able to manage energy is a skill worth having, but sadly most of us were taught very different skills, like how to manage data and information – things that seem real.

You can't see energy of course, but you can see the effect it has on its surroundings. Take for example, its effect on water. At one end of the scale there's the dramatic force of a tidal wave, and at the other end there's the eerie stillness of the doldrums. Both these extremes are wonderful to watch – from a distance. But for sailors, a tidal wave represents a quick, dramatic death, while the doldrums represent a slow, sad one.

Human beings are made up of about 70% water. To say that energy has no effect on us is a bit ridiculous. That's why we tend to stick to the safe zone in the middle. We're scared of the stuff at the edges – the rage of madness and the apathy of depression.

But the safe zone is boring, so we are drawn to people who are creative, spontaneous or slightly crazy. However, when their behaviour escalates to destructive anger or self-destructive despair we walk away. We create distance.

More importantly, when WE start to feel anger or despair, we create an internal distance... from ourselves.

And this distance can lead to depression. When we lose connection to ourselves, we become lonely... the kind of lonely that's often made worse by the presence of other people.

The energy world is the flip side of the real world, so when we inadvertently slip into it, other people may not understand. They say things like "Feeling lost and lonely? Put your party frock on, have a glass of wine, go out and be with people". But that feels crazy because the person you're lonely for is yourself; the person you've lost is yourself, and the kick ass personality you created to live in the real world, has collapsed like a pack of cards.

I'd burnt my bridges. I was trapped in limbo – unable to go back to the safe zone but lacking the resources to move forward. The real world didn't feel real anymore, and the energy world was an unchartered territory I had no control over.

How do we create momentum when life, for whatever reason, has become freeze framed by depression?

I trawled the internet looking for clues. These were my initial findings...

1. The Physical Stuff (for Your Body) – Medication

Medication definitely helps some people. In my research, many said it helped them manage the condition, not cure it. There are lots of different pills on the market, and everyone reacts differently. Each take a couple of weeks to kick in, so the whole process of trial and error can take a long time. I didn't feel drawn to go down this route.

Being a rebel, I have an inbuilt resistance to corporations. Pharmaceutical companies are huge money making machines whose sole purpose is profit for their shareholders, not the health of the general public. They think nothing of spending 250 million dollars lobbying to get their products on the market. Why? Because this sum represents only one per cent of their profits for the year. One per cent. When you hear the phrase "big business" make no mistake we're talking BIG business.

2. The Mental Stuff (for Your Mind) – Psychotherapy

The mind loves having problems to solve. It follows that finding a solution for depression is not high on its agenda. It prefers continuous searching.

Whenever anyone mentions psychotherapy to me, I think of Woody Allen. Fifty years of psychotherapy. Thousands of dollars. You may not have the time or the money. Again, it only helps manage, not cure, the condition. It's obvious really. Depression is an ailment of the mind – so how can it be fixed by the mind. Your mind is broken! It's hardly in a fit state to fix anything.

3. The Spiritual Stuff (for Your Soul) – New Age Self-Help

I did the most research here because this is after all the outer edge of the new paradigm, and I have a fondness for edges. I approached it with a healthy dose of cynicism, or as I like to call it DISCERNMENT. Stuff in here includes...

Energy healing – reiki and other treatments involving hands, hocus pocus and hieroglyphics.

Crystals – rocks with special powers.

Aromatherapy – scents with special powers.

Visualization – images with special powers.

Mantras – words with special powers.

You may have noticed a theme here. Namely that most of the special powers lie in external forces, whether that force is a Guru, or a piece of expensive chakra-aligning jewelry.

The only power that can transform life completely (as opposed to managing it) is the power inside. Unfortunately, this power is currently buried at the bottom of a black hole.

A piece of rose quartz won't help, any more than a hard hat and a canary.

If Body, Mind and Spirit are on a vertical axis, there is also a horizontal axis of left and right. These supply an Eastern and Western approach. You could also call these a Feminine and Masculine perspective.

4. The Eastern Holistic Stuff – Acupuncture and Ayurveda

There is no doubt, we are energetic beings. We're made of atoms, and atoms are mostly energy with a little bit of matter. Eastern medicine takes this into account. Rather than treating individual parts of the body separately, they treat the life force of the patient (their Chi or Prana) because if the life force is strong, then the body can heal itself.

This is a more feminine approach – as opposed to the masculine approach favored by the western world who like to nuke things or rip them out. *"Let's do this!... Illness is a hardware problem, a system malfunction. All that feminine stuff can come in later when we need hand-holding and cake."*

Depression is a place of almost zero life force, so anything that can improve this, like Acupuncture and Ayurveda can help a lot.

5. The Western John Wayne Stuff – Endurance

There are a lot of motivation books around at the moment. Many of them share the theme. *What doesn't kill you makes you strong.* Some are written by ex Soldiers who were beaten, tortured and put into solitary confinement for years. Their message is about strength of mind. They survived by making their will to live, stronger than their captors' lust for punishment.

When life has lost its meaning, it's not that helpful to be told that other people have survived situations a million times worse than the inability to get out of bed in the morning. These people sleep next to rats, on concrete. For the luxury of a bed, they'd probably cut off their right arm. With a Stanley knife.

This just makes you feel worse. Pathetic. Hopeless.

The feminine counterpart to this endurance test was described by John of the Cross, a 16th century monk, in his book *Dark Night of the Soul*. He was similarly captured and tortured. But rather than pit his will, against the will of his captors, he surrendered his will entirely... and became enlightened. Rather than fight reality with his mind, he entered the energy world, and found the power of his soul. With this power he was able to change reality, not only for himself, but for the thousands of people who read about his experience.

In order to achieve real freedom, sometimes we have to stop fighting and fall through the black hole to get to the other side. In more recent times, Nelson Mandela favored this strategy. As a rebellious, young man with a strong, sharp mind, he'd already tried the masculine approach. This certainly looked empowering, cool and sexy, but ultimately it was his feminine energy that brought about the end of Apartheid and changed the lives of millions of people.

So there I was under the duvet, trying to find a reason to get out of bed (attempting to visualize a vanilla latte). I wanted an attitude of gratitude #feelingblessed. I wanted to meditate #loveyoga. But in the end, the only thing that could entice me from the cocoon was the sacred union of espresso and syrup #sofucked.

Then I thought about writing this book.

Because you might be feeling the same.

THREE

The Problem with Words and Definitions

When I was young, this condition I have, wasn't called *Depression*, it was called a *Nervous Breakdown*. It implied that your nervous system had become derailed, so you weren't able to function in a normal way.

If the nervous system is the grid, along which the electricity of the body travels then depression does feel like a breakdown of this system. After all you feel no electricity inside, there is no force to direct your life, no fuel to propel you out of bed.

But nervous breakdown also implies that you are "nervous" which the dictionary describes as "apprehensive and highly excitable." That doesn't fit me. Right now, I can't remember how it feels to be excited by anything.

Words are hopeless.

Of course the older generation had a different context for the word *Depression*. It conjured up pictures of dustbowls in America, long lines at the bread store, longer lines at the ship-yards of anxious men trying to find work. That's why there is little support for depression these days.

"What d'you mean you're depressed?! Life is wonderful. Pull yourself together. Look on the bright side. Be more optimistic. Think of all those people living on a dollar a day. You're being SO self indulgent."

These are the words I'm sure many depressed people say to themselves. The mind wants action. *Do something constructive. Redecorate the living room. Learn to speak French. Run a marathon.* The voice of the mind is very masculine.

And yet, deeper down there is a very quiet voice that has a different kind of knowing. This voice says that happiness is not a reward for achieving things, it is our natural state. Just for being here. Just for turning up in the game of life. The voice of the soul is very feminine.

This quiet voice says that depression will never make sense to the mind, because it is not "of the mind", it is a sickness of the soul. Perhaps it's a kind of Cosmic Time Out. *"Stop! Let's have a re-think here!"* Perhaps it's an attempt by the soul to get itself heard. *"Enough with this kick ass personality, there are actually some things on MY agenda".* If this is true, I'd really like my soul to speak to me.

Silence.

My soul isn't speaking.

I wasn't completely stupid. Of course I knew my depression wasn't caused by the relationship breakdown. We'd been apart for three months. I was used to him *physically* not being there. But a *thought*, the realization that it really was over, had triggered something deeper – a feeling of powerlessness. I suddenly understood that I had no control over anything. All the control I thought I had, was an illusion. Maybe this feeling had always been there, but the potent mix of love and hope had given me immunity from it. Now that I was no longer protected, I felt its malevolent force dragging me downwards.

I had to pull myself together. I'd always been able to get things done in extreme circumstances, like lack of resources, food or sleep. I could work if I was ill, stressed or upset. I was a *"let's do this"* kind of person. Where did that energy come from? Where had it gone now?

The words "pull yourself together" are interesting, because what exactly are you pulling together? I suppose it's all the different aspects of yourself – body, mind, soul, emotions. Being a rebel I've always identified with my mind. My mind is who I think I am. I blame my body for not being the perfect body I want it to be. My emotions are flakey and cause me to do really inappropriate things, and I don't even know how to communicate with my soul because it doesn't use words.

I need to go back to the internet.

The prevailing research says that one in four people suffer mental health issues at some point in their life, but in reality this statistic must be more like four in four. We all have a body that goes out of balance and we all have a mind that goes out of balance as well. We don't normally ask people if they have ever had a physical health issue. It's a given that at some point they've had a cold, a virus or a sore throat.

In terms of physical health there's a scale of zero to 100% and we know roughly where we are on that scale. It varies from time to time.

Mental health is different because we're scared of it. We make it black and white. Either we suffer from mental health issues... or we don't. Most of us cling firmly to the "don't" camp. We avert our eyes from crazy drunks on the pavement and we roll our eyes at people who burst into tears at the slightest provocation.

We hate things that are difficult to define, which is why we love it when we have a diagnosis with a proper word. "I've got tonsillitis! We say this proudly to work colleagues, the sub text being "see I wasn't just being a bit pathetic, I have something that has a proper name."

Things in the energy world either don't have a name, or they have an inadequate one that covers way too many bases. Deep down, everything is a bunch of vibrating atoms. That's why we like to stay on the surface level, where things look more real. Then we can talk about them using the same frame of reference – WORDS.

But at its core, everything is energy. We are connected. If the world becomes unbalanced, (and right now the world is very unbalanced) we can stick our fingers in our ears and look away, but deep down we can feel it, because we're connected to each other. Perhaps this is a factor for the huge increase in depression.

Some things on the planet understand a balanced, connected system. Humans are not amongst them. We think we're the smartest thing on the planet because we have an intellect. Using this "evolutionary upgrade" we've made amazing progress in technology, engineering and medicine.

But now things are going wrong...

Technology has made us more and more disconnected from the living world. Many people spend so much time on line, that their virtual world is more real than the actual one.

Engineering has changed our relationship to the environment. Food is nuked and genetically modified. The earth has become a garbage heap from the by products of industry.

Medicine has become big business because bad health is a money spinner. Pharmaceutical companies have a marketing budget larger than the GDP of some countries.

Relying purely on our intellect, we've created a world that's a bit crazy to say the least.

Animals don't have an intellect but at least they are more balanced than we are. They can act as an individual (when searching for supper) and they can act as a species (when migrating south for the winter). Unlike humans (who are focused on self-interest), they have the ability to be both separate and part of a whole, SIMULTANEOUSLY.

Even plants have this system. Trees are connected by an intricate electrical system that links their roots to the tiny membranes of soil fungus, which cover miles of distance. This is a bit like a non-verbal tree telephone system.

We have lost our connection to the whole, because we love being an individual, but we retain a need to connect to SOMETHING, so we project this need...

Either indiscriminately *"Notice me, one thousand random people on Facebook"* or with extreme focus *"Notice me, one person I'm in love with"*.

Obviously there's nothing wrong with my ability to focus.

Having a clever mind is good, up to a point. But for all the new problems we are facing these days, we need a different kind of intelligence – an intelligence with greater power and fewer words.

So I set off on a quest to find it.

FOUR

The First Workshop and My Bad Attitude

I'm on my way to a new-age, self-empowerment style workshop. I won't say what it's called because for the purpose of this book, they are all very similar (though of course the marketing blurb will say in **bold print** or BLOCK CAPS that they are exclusive, and different from everything else out there because their processes are **unique** and GROUNDBREAKING).

I hate marketing, but I need help.

The main aim of these workshops is twofold.

1   A changed mindset, from negative to positive. With better thinking we can reframe any situation and find the pearl in the oyster. There are no problems, just challenges. There are no catastrophes only life lessons. It IS possible to make a silk purse out of a

sow's ear. Science has discovered neuroplasticity, which means our brains are elastic and can learn new ways to think. As depression is a very negative mind set, finding new ways to think about things is a very good idea.

2 A changed perspective from head to heart. "Do what you love" and "Follow your bliss" are mantras that have been bandied around since the sixties. Passion comes from the heart not the mind. Ideas come from the mind, but without the passion to carry them through, they remain just ideas. Passion creates energy to do things and as I barely have enough energy to tie my shoelaces at the moment, this is exactly what I need. (This is not a joke – I look at my trainers wistfully, then choose the boots with the zip up the side. I really cannot be arsed with laces).

I arrive in a small rural town that seems to sell nothing practical (like vanilla lattes, nice pens or phone chargers). Instead the shops are full of dream catchers, tarot cards and Goddess figurines. New age aphorisms are EVERYWHERE – on cards, coffee mugs, cushion covers. Ancient philosophies are reduced to sound bites and bits of embroidery.

Getting away from the city is pretty much a pre-requisite if you are to succeed in "getting out of your head and into your heart". The pace is slower. The people are nicer. Personally I hate both slow and nice. They tend NOT to go with a word I like better – efficient. If there was one place designed to take me as far away from my heart as possible, it was this place.

Stop being so cynical! People are lovely. Life is good.

I enter the workshop venue, register and go straight to the book display. Books are a lifeline in situations like these, because they give you a point of focus. A point of focus equals calm. Without this you might run for the door, because it can feel like you've arrived on a strange planet. Repeat attendees greet each other theatrically and engage in deep meaningful hugs that seem to go on for a very long time. Sometimes they also make eye contact while hugging. The intention is to "really see" the other person so they feel validated, but to an outsider, it just looks a bit creepy.

The workshop begins. The repeat attendees have already been in the room and, like German tourists with beach towels, have placed bags and cardigans on the seats near the front. The facilitator walks up and down making meaningful eye contact with the first few rows of the audience. They blush and start to glow with the radiance of "being seen". It's a bit like a Kajagoogoo concert.

Clearly I'm very much still in my head, because I haven't thought about Kajagoogoo since 1983, which is about as far away from the present moment as you can get. In a sea of rock and roll and heavy metal, Kajagoogoo were the only "pop" band I worked on, so the memory of them is really clear.

Whereas the rock and roll fans watched their idols with respect, and the heavy metal fans mirrored theirs with head rocking frenzy, "pop" fans favored a different approach. By the time Limahl (the lead singer) walked on stage, half the front row had already fainted in anticipation. The other half, gazed up in a kind of rapture. Dilated pupils. Open mouths. Tears streaming down their face. It was as if the Archangel Gabriel had descended with a personal letter from the Almighty.

Why? How? WTF?

Clearly all this love and passion is a projection. The energy was not created by Limahl himself. Nobody really knew who he was. It was created by an idea, a *thought* in the mind of the teenage girls. This energy then escalated, bounced between each of them, gathering more and more momentum until it pulled them higher into a state of collective consciousness. Is this consciousness similar to the one felt by mystics in their divine union with God?

What is the connection between the highly disciplined soul of the mystic and the unconscious psyche of the teenage girl?

I am suddenly aware that there's a change of atmosphere in the workshop. The noise level has increased. People are talking and gathering into groups for some sort of exercise. I clearly haven't been listening AT ALL. Luckily the person sitting next to me wants to include me in her group so I don't have to feel the awkwardness of asking to join one.

Self-help workshops always involve a lot of "sharing". When you add this word to "kind" and "slow" it is a recipe for monumental levels of irritation. In an effort to be kind, people begin sentences with "I know this is my projection but..." and then go on to be really judgmental about whoever has wronged them. They do this using an unfeasible amount of unnecessary words and heartfelt pauses, so the process is very, very slow.

On no account can you voice what you're actually thinking. (Something along the lines of "I get it. Cut to the chase. I'm really bored") because the person won't feel "heard" which is a crime equal to not being "seen". And so a ritual that's designed to be honest and accountable... often isn't.

In these circumstances, it is very difficult to stay present and "in the now" but I force my mind back from the 1980s (by this time I'd moved on to *Dexy's Midnight Runners)* and I look around the room.

The exercise we had to do involved introducing ourselves, discussing the role we played in our original family, and getting feedback from the new family we were surrounded by.

Basically we are all born with natural desires – you could say these are the desires of the soul, because the mind is not fully formed at that time. However, as soon as we develop a mind, we replace these natural instincts with the kind of desires that get us attention. We start to adapt. Looking at the role we played in our original family, can help us remember what bits of ourselves we exaggerated, and what bits we threw away.

Then we can discover our true self.

I am bone tired, but I do want to do this. I have to find my "true self" as a matter of urgency, because my current self has a strange urge to reach for a shotgun.

I'm now thinking of Ernest Hemingway, and wondering how long he thought about things before putting a bullet through his head. Did he count down from ten, or three or did he just go for it.

Please stop. This is not helping.

I look around my group and try to imagine who each of these people could represent from my original family. I fail to come up with anything. If this was my family, I'd have already left to join the circus.

There are six of them. Names are difficult to keep track of, so I'll identify each with some sort of feature.

1 Beardy Man. Apparently he used to be very shut down but after a lot of self-help he has now reformed himself, re-kindled romance with his wife and is very happy. He demonstrates his new found joy by adopting a very soppy expression when anybody speaks (he REALLY listens) and by placing the palm of his hand over his heart, a gesture that seems to imply he's so touched by who-ever is speaking, that his heart might leap from his chest if not contained.

2 Goddess Woman. Unfortunately there's always one in a work-shop. These are often evolved versions of Ladies Who Lunch. They've replaced the martinis and shoulder pads, with green smoothies and floaty dresses. They don't wear jewels for adorn-ment, but for protection against evil forces. They know the properties of each stone so have to "tune in" to the prevailing energies in the cosmos before getting dressed in the morning.

3 Angry Woman. She has been taken advantage of by men her whole life. She's the original feminist, from back in the day, when

31

men were the devil and it was all about gender competition. She listens to arguments about how it's now all about masculine and feminine ENERGY. Beardy Man says he is a feminist, and he's definitely a man (laughter all round as people concur). I am not so sure. If it is all about energy, then what defines a man is his masculine energy and looking at Beardy Man, I can't detect any masculine energy whatsoever.

4 Bonkers Woman. She won't leave home without casting her astrology chart, the i-ching and her set of hand carved runes that have been infused with special properties and healing powers by a Peruvian shaman. Her speech is littered with mystical references to planetary constellations, astral planes and akashic records. She usually channels somebody epic like Mary Magdalene or Joan of Arc, and for a fee will bring forth some of their ancient wisdom to help solve present day problems. I don't know if Mary and Joan get some kind of intellectual property rights for this. It's a bit of a murky area.

5 (And 6) The new-age couple. The ones who are always looking meaningfully into each others eyes. They are on a quest to deepen their relationship, heal their pain and grow in ever increasing levels of intimacy and trust. She usually looks like his mother (she's not older, she just smiles a lot in that motherly kind of way). I have been guilty of adopting this expression in the presence of CHILDREN, but this man is at least 40 so it's a bit cringe making. He meanwhile usually looks like he's been dragged here on some kind of punishment-reward premise. He will agree to change his old alpha male ways in exchange for the promise of really hot tantric sex.

And there's me. Suddenly feeling quite normal. Though still very, very tired and deprived of my best friend (triple shot vanilla latte).

FIVE

The Seemingly Random Audition for the Roles We Play

First we talk about the relationship with our Fathers. Some of the group described fathers who were distant, critical, or aggressive. But in the main, fathers were just guilty of insufficient praise, an inability to play, and a reluctance to read bed-time stories.

This old version of fatherhood is a distant memory for Beardy man who is number one cheerleader for his little bunnies and loves nothing more than to read *The Tiger Who Came To Tea* for the hundredth time – still doing all the voices and never turning over two pages at once accidentally on purpose.

Then of course we had to discuss everyone's relationship to their Mother. What damage they caused!

The Goddess's mother was a Catholic martyr who failed to role model any kind of healthy sexuality to her daughter. This caused terrible confusion. The Goddess had adopted all manner of dysfunctional behaviours from repressing her sexuality (chastity and bulimia) to exaggerating it (rampant promiscuity and cocaine). Now her life was about realizing the Divine Feminine within and self-love. After all, "if you can't love yourself you can't love anybody."

I'm sure the term self-love started out with good intentions – in a sort of "I really fucked that situation up, but I'm only human, so I'm going to forgive myself instead of beating myself up 24/7, because then at least I'll be able to get some work done." This REALLY GOOD IDEA has kind of morphed into narcissistic self-indulgence. If the Divine Feminine is energy, which is INVISIBLE, then surely there's no need to check for its presence in the mirror – something the Goddess does ALL THE TIME.

Angry woman's mother on the other hand was harsh and critical. She pushed her daughter to achieve academically because she didn't want her to be subservient to men. Angry woman dedicated her life to her career – but still she wasn't on the same pay grade as her male counterparts, who relished the chance to put her down, make misogynist comments and take credit for her ideas. I don't know where I am with this one. On the one hand I can sympathize because inequality is CLEARLY WRONG. On the other hand, there's a small voice that says "Jesus, lighten up. It's no wonder men treat you like this, you're a pain in the arse." This is not a very sisterly, or spiritual thought, so I have to send it back to hang out with *Dexy's Midnight Runners* while I turn my attention to...

Bonkers woman. Her mother sounded more like Germaine Greer. Politically active in her youth, she campaigned tirelessly to save the environment, refusing to cut or die her long white hair. The Goddess sighed with envy hearing this, saying how wonderful it must have been, to have such an empowered "wise woman" as a role model (instead of the Catholic door mat she had to contend with). Bonkers disagreed. It wasn't wonderful at all. Her mother was too busy fighting causes to be around much. She dreamed of having a mother who made jam tarts and sewed little dresses for her dolls. That's when she started to retreat into her own world of invented friends and fairies.

The aliens from other planets followed shortly after.

My Dad and Mum were pretty normal as far as I can tell. They were Catholic, meaning Dad was the Patriarch with the strong work ethic and Mum had a degree in self-sacrifice. But I wasn't traumatized by my childhood, I just can't remember much of it. I also don't remember the plots of books I read a few years ago, and my childhood happened a long time before that.

I understand the general idea behind retracing our steps – it's where all our patterns begin. As babies, we are hard wired to find two things... attention and love. Attention gives us proof that we exist and love makes us feel good.

Perhaps I wandered through childhood in a bit of a trance, and only woke up when things became more real. By that time I was completely in control. I'd become a fully fledged rebel who didn't need anything. Since falling down a black hole, I seem to have regressed into a pre-trance state. All I have to do is pull up an image of my boyfriend to feel a twist in my stomach that seems to say *"NOTICE ME! LOVE ME!"*

I am pathetic. Deep down.

My ego rallies and tries to re-assemble some form of personality by judging everyone in the room.

I'm not pathetic. I'm better than her, more interesting than him, definitely less boring than them.

Stop it! Give me a break. Please stop. Just for 5 minutes. I'm exhausted.

I try to re-engage with the workshop, where the facilitator is now describing the various strategies we adopt to get our needs met. As a child, if we did something well (for example, run fast, do a funny dance or add some numbers together correctly) we get attention. This is like manna from heaven to the child, who does it again, and again, and again. Eventually because of this repetition we get quite good at the behaviour and it becomes a role.

We know when it has gone from a natural expression of our inner creativity to a role, because it becomes something we HAVE to do whether we feel like it or not. It has become part of our identity. "This is Johnny he's a whizz at math. Meet Sarah, a gifted dancer. Tom is such a clown."

It's not enough that we are Johnny, Sarah or Tom, we must have some kind of identity because this enables further interaction. "Oh I was hopeless at math when I was at school. I've always loved the ballet! Your mummy must be so proud of you."

You could say we need an identity, because we don't know how else to start a conversation about ourselves. But it's a bit of a tragedy when this identity becomes a role, because we end up living life according to a recipe instead of the spontaneous, creative expression of who we are. It's also a disaster waiting to happen. After all, what if Johnny is replaced by a computer, Sarah breaks a leg or Tom dies on stage? You just know depression is waiting in the wings.

We are illiterate when it comes to describing who we are, so it's no wonder we struggle with choosing the various ways we could express it.

There are lots of adults in self-help workshops who say things like "I've been a lawyer all my life and I have no idea why. I hate it. It's just that one thing led to another." What they are describing is the way a natural aptitude got turned, too quickly, into a role. Once this is discovered the person sometimes leaves and builds a school in Kenya. Or they stay, because the pension is good and they're scared to start again.

What's clear to me is that I have no idea what my real self is. If I'm talking to Beardy man who is a bit needy, I'm an independent, kick ass person. If I'm talking to Goddess woman who is searching for her soul mate, I decide men are over rated and I don't need one. If I'm talking to Angry woman, I LOVE ALL MEN. If I'm talking to Bonkers woman, I'm a new-age cynic, but I know, that outside these walls, if I met a group of arrogant business men, I'd morph into an astral travelling, crystal wearing high priestess.

In the blink of an eye.

I'm just a reaction to whatever's around me. I have negative approval seeking syndrome. I don't want the love and approval of other people, I just want it from one person – my boyfriend.

I look at Couple woman. Was I as annoying as this when I was in a relationship? Wanting more. Wanting him to change. Wanting him to prefer my company over that of his computer.

I would never actually SAY any of those things of course... But I did think them.

Thought is energy. Really creative people can feel the energy because they're intuitive. It doesn't matter what you say or don't say. It's about what your thoughts are saying.

I should have been more careful.

And now it's too late.

No!

My ego rallies again, as it remembers Beardy man's story of his near divorce and subsequent reconciliation. It was a *"Tale of Two Energies."* His wife was needy, while he was independent. They were positive and negative forces. She was awash in a sea of emotions, feeling everything. He was on a camel in the desert, feeling nothing. Then she left him, and it reversed. He started feeling all the neediness. Meanwhile she became independent and attractive again. It's just energy. It doesn't belong to anyone. We take turns. It's all about learning to play nicely on the see-saw.

Perhaps if I really feel my needy feelings and let them go, my boyfriend will sense something different and come back. I'm a high achiever, I could feel ALL the needy feelings, his and mine. He can stay at the top of the see-saw if he wants... as long as I get to stay in the same playground.

I clutch this strand of hope and try to pull it slowly towards me. I am George Clooney in *Gravity*, trying to get back to the space ship, wishing I hadn't used up all my air supply singing and generally larking around.

In the energy world, everyone wants contradictory things.

They want love and bonding and they also want independence and freedom. It's just a matter of finding the sweet spot between the two. This also applies to life in general. People want security (a steady job, their own home) and they want unpredictability (a job that's a bit challenging, a house with potential). Again there's a ratio. Too much security is boring, too much unpredictability is frightening.

Working out the ratio is something the mind likes to do, but an element can come from childhood, which is why the facilitator is focusing there. A smothering parent could create a child who needs space. A distant parent might produce a child that's desperate for validation. Critical parents could lead a child to become a perfectionist, or a rebel, depending on which role they choose...

1 I'll be really perfect, then people will love me.

2 Fuck you, I don't need anyone's approval.

In this way the rebel creates attention, which is their safe substitute for love.

My boyfriend and I were both rebels. We sung from the same hymn sheet. But life seeks harmonies, not *Johnny One Note,* so the relationship pulled up the repressed bits. The minor chords. He needed more space. I needed more connection, causing him to require even more space... and the vicious circle continued. Until it broke.

I'm tired and I want to go home. People are milling about smiling and being positive. I look across at Beardy man who's in deep conversation with Angry woman. I wonder if it's compulsory for emotional intelligence to look so soppy.

Stop it! That's not helpful or spiritual. It's cynical.
The opposite of sincerity.

But what is sincerity? The dictionary describes it as honesty, freedom from deceit. If this is how I feel, then surely trying NOT to feel it is deceiving myself.

Perhaps that's why so much new age philosophy doesn't work. Our conscious mind is going around loving everyone, feeling grateful and creating a positive future but our subconscious one is having a field day in the opposite direction. The subconscious part is much bigger, so it wins every time.

I'm ashamed of my thoughts. They're vicious and unkind. Both to other people, and to myself. It's no wonder my soul is keeping quiet.

So where does this leave me now that the workshop is breaking for lunch? As Joan would say (Joan Crawford, not Joan of Arc!) "This ain't my first time at the rodeo." I've studied this stuff. I know my subconscious patterns.

But obviously I don't know my unconscious ones. I'm living a different story now. One in which I went to sleep in Kansas and woke up in Oz. Nothing feels real any more.

The others suggest having lunch together. We are a family group after all. I don't want to be distant. I actually hate feeling like this, so I force a smile and agree that this is a splendid suggestion.

SIX

Sugar Fix
– Name Your Poison

Lunch for me is always a stressful affair because I have a really bad relationship with food. This relationship is so dysfunctional, it makes my relationship with people look positively enlightened. It started as long ago as I can remember. In fact my earliest memory, around the age of 9 involved keeping the shilling by mother gave me for school lunch, borrowing (without asking, so more like temporarily stealing) a bicycle from the school shed, and cycling as fast as possible to the sweet shop where I would buy a whole box of Maltesers.

This to me was a mixture of decadence and practicality. Other children, normal children, would buy an individual packet of Maltesers, not a family sized box, so this was hedonism on a grand scale. But at the same time, given the choice between proper adult food, and food that makes you childishly happy, who wouldn't opt for the family sized box. With my super rational mind, I reasoned that the only thing stopping everyone from doing this was the fear of getting caught.

Since then I have had what is euphemistically called "a sweet tooth" but what is more realistically called a full blown sugar addiction. I know people with "a sweet tooth". It means they sometimes opt for a starter and a desert rather than a main meal. It does NOT mean that they substitute the starter and main meal for three deserts.

After school came the career in rock and roll. Work that is carried out "on location" (eg music venue/film set) is usually accompanied by "catering." After all, you are either in the middle of nowhere, or you barely have enough time to pee so "popping out to the shops" is not an option.

Caterers (Bless them!) like to make sure you eat whenever you're hungry. This might not coincide with meal times. Also when it's actual meal times, you might be up a lighting rig or trying to understand a box office spreadsheet. Because of this, they helpfully lay out baskets and baskets of lovely sweet things – chocolate bars and snacks in a size called "fun size" (because they bring JOY to all who consume them). I think they were originally designed for children's lunch boxes, but the fact that you can easily stuff half a dozen down each leg of your astronaut suit is an added bonus.

By the time I was a proper adult, with a serious career in marketing, my sugar addiction was firmly in place. I've never been able to cure this addiction, I manage it – sometimes reasonably well, sometimes not at all. Managing it entails delaying the chocolate fix as late in the day as possible. After dinner represents a good day. Pain au Chocolat at dawn, not so good. Because once the sugar monster is woken up, it is insatiable and you have to keep feeding it all day.

So now it's lunch and I'm standing in a café in front of red velvet cake, hazelnut meringues and chocolate brownies. There's must also be other stuff because I can hear the group members requesting pumpkin soup and vegetarian lasagna, but I'm transfixed, like

Mowgli in the Jungle Book, cartwheels in my eyes, hypnotized, not by Kaa but by cake.

I pay for the red velvet and a cappuccino and at the last minute casually mention a chocolate brownie "to eat later". This implies the tea break in the middle of the afternoon, as opposed to the reality (immediately after the red velvet cake).

Of all the addictions, sugar is the least glamorous because in addition to the self-hatred that comes with any addiction, you have to deal with contempt from the outside world. It's bad enough admitting that a random substance has more power over you than your own mind, but when it also makes you fat, you can't even hide the fact. Like adulterous women in medieval times, who had to walk around with a giant "A" on their frocks, fat announces to the world that you're losing the war against your drug of choice.

This is a shame because it is the least anti-social drug. Unlike alcoholics, people with a sugar addiction don't rampage through the streets at closing time, picking fights, smashing windows and vomiting. Their behaviour is secret, sad, and far less flamboyant. They do things like offering to wash up so they can finish the half eaten deserts others have left. They creep downstairs in the middle of the night to eat chocolate, then wracked with guilt, drive miles to a gas station to replace it before other people wake up. They struggle to concentrate at meetings because someone put a plate of biscuits on the table and even though nobody else is eating them, they can't possibly take a third, because everyone will notice.

Unlike heroin, sugar is cheap, freely available and mass marketed by an unscrupulous food industry. Yet despite this, there is no sympathy for the sugar addict. There aren't even any fringe benefits, like being able to fit into a pair of skinny jeans. This addiction is neither poignant or poetic.

Alcoholics and recreational drug users have more artistic associations. Richard Burton, Elizabeth Taylor, Dylan Thomas, Tennessee Williams, Truman Capote, F. Scott Fitzgerald, Ernest Hemingway,

Steven Tyler, Whitney Houston, Amy Whitehouse, the list is end-less. Not all alcoholics are poets, some of them are just drunks, but they have our sympathy because they seem to be fighting a noble battle.

The battle against food isn't noble. Even though studies show that sugar is as addictive as heroin. That can't be right, I hear you say, because some people don't get addicted to sugar. Well, some people don't get addicted to heroin. If they're ill, they're treated in hospital for weeks or months with all kinds of opiates, but when they get out, they don't rush straight down the corner to score an 8-ball. They go home and have a nice cup of tea.

We're all sitting down now at a big circular table with a gingham cloth and mismatched crockery. Angry woman looks at my cake with incomprehension. Apparently she has not eaten sugar, gluten or dairy for two years, so to have all three on the same plate must be some kind of death wish. Goddess woman gives me a conspiratorial grin and says "enjoy!" She has no fear of carbs, but having "tuned in to her body" it told her that the quinoa and kale salad was just the ticket.

I make a mental note to have one of these conversations with my body. Something along the lines of WHY OH WHY BODY? WHAT IS IT WITH YOU? CAN'T YOU AT LEAST TRY TO GET WITH THE KALE THING? I have a feeling this conversation will end with sulking, then possibly ice cream.

Still, after the sugar hit of the cake, I feel marginally better. These are not bad people. They are actually really lovely. In light of the morning conversations, I look around the table through a different lens, like Alice surveying a tea party of very diverse characters.

I can imagine Beardy man as a small geeky boy, trying to be liked, but always slightly out of step with his friends. Perhaps he has a Thomas the Tank lunch box, when the other boys have moved on to Mutant Ninja Turtles. They ridicule him. He doesn't cry, at least not straight away, but later, under his equally inappropriate Winnie the

SUGAR FIX – NAME YOUR POISON

Pooh duvet cover, which now offers both succor and shame in equal measure. I experience the dart go in and feel a surge of compassion.

Then there's Goddess woman. I can see her dancing in front of an oval mirror, tossing her head coquettishly, mini boobs created from rolled up socks down the front of her vest, the look of horror on her Mother's face as she scolds her for being such a hussy. The little flicker of the curious, emerging soul snuffed out, in a cold pious wind.

Then Angry woman. That one's easy. Walking home from school, basking in the glow from her teacher's praise, holding a report card filled with A's, and B's. Greeted by a mother too consumed by recent evidence of her husband's fecklessness to pay attention. Then later, when things were quiet, presenting the peace offering, the written proof of her worthiness. Watching her mother's critical eyes skip past the A grades to focus purely on the Bs.

Bonkers woman was just born at the wrong time. In these days of Harry Potter, Vampire Diaries and Lord of the Rings, a fey child with a vivid imagination would be celebrated, not left to languish, lonely in her room. Culture is a very fickle thing.

And the Couple. Even they don't seem so ridiculous now. Perhaps if I'd worked harder on my relationship, instead of relying on spontaneity and fate, I'd still be in a relationship. Couple man, was recounting a funny anecdote about his partner, eyes twinkling with love and respect. It was sweet. I remembered when my boy-friend looked at me this way, then before I could stop myself, I started making a different kind of comparison. The man sitting opposite was archetypal new-age. Long, thin grey hair tied back in a pony tail, dull skin, ugly jumper, badly fitting jeans. Physical stuff is superficial. It shouldn't matter, but the one good thing about falling in love with a narcissistic man is impeccable grooming.

Don't think about him. Don't think about him. Don't think about him. Too late. Tears have already started to pool and one of them is trickling down my face. Couple woman and Goddess woman are already giving me their full attention. After some feeble attempts to change the subject, I admit that I am struggling somewhat with a broken heart.

"Men!" exclaims Angry woman, adopting a Boadicea like expression. Couple woman gives me a look of such compassion that I feel ashamed. I can hardly say these tears were partly brought about by contemplating the unattractiveness of her husband.

I am so shallow.

"He obviously wasn't *the one*" Goddess Woman proclaims. "Let him go and your true soul mate will appear, one who's worthy of you." Seeing as how spectacularly unworthy I feel right now, this is not positive news. The cosmic dating service is probably lining me up with Quasimodo.

Meanwhile I am aware that Beardy man is subjecting me to one of his deep, meaningful stares. I look up and make eye contact. Being on the receiving end is less cringe making than observing it third hand. "I don't think it's over," he says portentously. "It doesn't feel over to me". This is the feedback I really want. Beardy man has transformed in my eyes from wet hippy to ancient seer of Merlin like proportions. I feel really guilty for having judged him earlier in the day, and now want him to be my best friend.

Everything is energy. If I successfully change my energy, my boyfriend will feel it. We are atoms that are entangled. When he senses the return of my power, he will want to be with me again.

Beardy man is right. It is not over. The fat lady is not singing. But if I don't stop eating cake, I might soon be joining her on stage.

As we leave the café, we pass an old woman sitting on a bench. I give her the chocolate brownie. I sincerely hope she's #feelingblessed.

SEVEN

The Patterns in the Low Frequency World

In the afternoon session, we move from roles to patterns – the dysfunctional patterns of masculine and feminine energy. We are well and truly in the energy world now.

Because energy is invisible, Carl Jung described it in terms of archetypes. An archetype is a kind of stencil, a template through which energy flows. This template gives us something we can all agree on, because energy is notoriously difficult to language.

The archetypes associated with dysfunctional feminine energy are:

The Victim – she tries to get power through self-pity, drama, learned dependency and the ability to make other people feel guilty.

The Martyr – like a victim on steroids. The martyr doesn't need to do sighs and eye rolling to get noticed, her energy is so strong you can feel it as soon as you enter the room.

The Damsel – is scared of power so wants to be rescued and then live vicariously through someone else's power. She's needy, but gets away with it because she manages to look pretty while doing so. With little energy to run her own life, she is easily pulled into the orbit of other people – particularly men who have abundant amounts of power. The Damsel is addicted to the feelings of being in love – or more correctly addicted to the thoughts that create the feelings of love. Her beloved isn't around very often, so most of the romance goes on in her head.

The Prostitute – tries to negotiate for power through a trade off. On one level this might be "I give you my body in exchange for money" but these days it's more likely to be "I won't tell any-body you're fiddling the books if you give me the promotion" or "I'll stay in this loveless marriage because I don't want to leave this big house".

While these are not attractive, it's important to remember evolution. We all want the power to lead our own lives. For thousands of years women haven't had any means (other than the ones mentioned above) to get power. A few hundred years ago, women were burnt at the stake for making herbal medicines. Only men (with their butcher's knives and blood sucking leeches) could claim the power to heal the sick. Only men could interpret the "voice" of God and be his intermediary on earth.

In many parts of the world women STILL don't have the power to make their own decisions about who to marry or what to wear. They can't vote, can't drive and can't complain if they're beaten up for some mild misdemeanor, like burning the toast.

Living in a country where a legitimate response to absent-mind-edness would be "make your own fucking toast" it's easy for us to forget the legacy we've inherited from our ancestors. That's why we often have no sympathy for women who engage in dysfunctional female power dynamics. We want to distance ourselves from them. In my past, I created so much distance that I successfully gained access to the boy's club. But the behaviour over there, is just as bad, it's merely a different kind of dysfunction.

The archetypes associated with dysfunctional masculine energy are:

The Bully – he gains power through aggression. Bullies hate victims, but their behaviour creates the very thing they hate. The bully needs a victim in the same way the victim needs a bully. They have to co-exist otherwise they lose their ability to exist at all.

The Don Juan – gains power through sex and seduces everyone, both male and female. He doesn't necessary act it out, he's just very liberal in the sexual charisma department. Sexual energy comes from the 2nd chakra, the same place creativity comes from, so in a sense this is prostituting creative energy by expressing it in its lowest form. Don Juan is only interested in conquest, so all the sex tends to be the "below the belt" sort, not the high flying tantric kind. It's all about the numbers – quantity of conquests, not quality of devotion.

The Bad Geek – in the old days this might have been the hermit, only he's swopped his cave for a computer. He gains his power through technology. Everything is great as long as he doesn't have to interact with any human beings. He likes virtual friends (social media) virtual sex (porn) and virtual aggression (trolling).

The Cowboy – power by being cool, aloof, and looking like he has his shit together. Always accompanied by a prop of some kind. In the old days this was cigarettes and a horse, these days it's more likely to be sunglasses and a black Prada turtleneck. This is independence on steroids – the polar opposite of the dependent damsel, so they kind of attract each other. There's never a long term love match as the cowboy always has an escape plan – in the past, something fast and four legged, these days more likely to be metal and made by Mercedes.

Writing this down has reminded me how much of a damsel I became. Because it happened slowly, I wasn't aware. It was only on a cold railway station, late at night that she finally emerged. But my boyfriend had obviously sensed her hiding. That's why he left. Underneath my astronaut suit there's an organza dress with a high waist and very big sleeves.

Damn.

The afternoon workshop session follows the same format as the morning. I'm feeling a bit numb and really regretting the decision to give away the chocolate brownie. The facilitator is drawing a triangle on a white board. I know this bit. He is about to explain the root cause of many relationship problems – the Oedipus conspiracy.

If you haven't come across this one, I'll give you my version of it.

When babies are born they don't sense their individuality. Like the trees in the forest, they are connected to everything. *Ah! The bliss of true connection!* They watch their hand moving, unaware that it is actually their hand. They have no sense of ownership, no sense of subject-object, no boundaries. They come from a high frequency environment to a low frequency one. That's why people often refer to them as little angels.

Pretty soon, however, they adapt to this low frequency world, the world where things are separate, where we can't be two things simultaneously (separate individual AND connected to the whole of life). We have to choose.

"No," the soul says, "stay at the high frequency and you can be both!"

But the force of gravity is strong and the child is weak, so she drops to the lower frequency and sees that things are separate. There's a Mum and a Dad. This fall from grace is marked by the first thought, which is "If I'm separate from everything and I'm disconnected from the source of life, how on earth am I going to get my needs met?"

Things that are connected to the source of life, don't have to ask this question. They trust that their needs will be met by a higher intelligence – the kind of intelligence that came up with really smart stuff... like photosynthesis.

Things that are separated from their source, on the other hand, experience FEAR. When we experience fear, we look for something alternative to attach to. If the child attaches to the mother, they exclude the father. If they attach to the father, they exclude the mother. If they attach to neither, they exclude themselves.

This is the first rule of the low frequency world – THERE ARE WINNERS AND LOSERS.

The first thought we have, is quickly followed by our first feeling. Because this feeling is associated with winning and losing, it's either guilt or heartbreak.

If you lose, you feel heartbroken. If you win, someone else loses, so you feel guilty.

At the root of all our patterns is this simple dynamic of competition. It's the first law of a low frequency world.

The second law of the low frequency world doesn't have a word, so I'll make one up – triangulation. Everything we experience is divided into three – Subject Object and Space between.

As soon as we are able to speak WORDS, we go to primary school to develop our mind further and learn about SENTENCES. Here, there is a subject, an object and a verb in the space between. For example, "I ride my bike" – the subject is "I" the object is "bike" and the verb is "ride".

Our mind is always focused on the object –that's how it sees everything... as objects. Because of this, it thinks all the joy is in the object. *If only I had a new bike I'd be happy.* But a new bike becomes boring very quickly. All the joy is in the riding. The joy is in the verb.

The joy is ALWAYS in the space between.

Our soul (the only thing that can experience happiness) lives in the space between things, because it's an energy, not an object. Unfortunately, I live in my mind. It's a more familiar territory than my soul. I followed my mind's strategy for happiness – goal setting, competition and achievement. External things.

Perhaps this depression is not a problem that needs fixing. Perhaps it's an initiation into the soul. An invitation to explore space. Inner space.

In space, there are no words.

And no-one can hear you scream.

It's not for the faint hearted.

EIGHT

Changing the Pattern by Occupying the Space Between

Cognitive Behaviour Therapy seems to be the current therapy du jour for depressed people. Thoughts create feelings and feelings lead to behaviour. To change behaviour, it makes sense to retrace these steps – become aware of how you're feeling, discover the thoughts that created the feeling, then change those thoughts into better thoughts. It's simple but difficult to do because the way we think is quite entrenched.

Workshops use various tools for discovering old thought patterns. These techniques aim to externalize the thoughts, so they can be stopped, analyzed and changed into better, more positive, more REALISTIC thought patterns.

The facilitator pulls up the new-age couple to demonstrate the Oedipal conspiracy. Let's call them Tom and Kate. As a child, Kate was a Daddy's girl. When she walked in the room Dad's face lit up. This was Kate's first experience of power. After all, this didn't happen when Mum walked in. Kate won (good feeling) but felt guilty (bad feeling). She repressed the guilt. Obviously. Who wants to feel that?

In adult life, Kate won Tom's heart (winning = good feeling) and they had a great time dating. There was Kate, Tom and the space between them. All the joy was in the space. There was excitement, curiosity, anticipation, creativity. (Romance can be highly creative). Once they got married, there was a lot less space. They were in close proximity all the time. So, two things happened...

1 The Space contained all the erotic charge, so now that they were closer, there was less space, less charge, therefore less sex.

2 As the bonding between them increased, it allowed all the repressed stuff to come to the surface (guilt = bad feeling). Kate started projecting her relationship with her father onto Tom, (Eugh! Oedipal!) so now she certainly didn't feel like having sex with him.

In the workshop, Kate and Tom have to pick members of the audience to represent their original blueprint for bonding – Mum, Dad and the child version of themselves. Then they pick people to represent abstract things – the energy of guilt, the love of independence and the fear of intimacy. Finally they pick each other to represent True Love.

There are now lots of people standing in the centre of the room, pretending to be either characters in a play or abstract concepts in an avant-garde play.

Kate walks slowly towards her "father". It's clear she adores him, but when she reaches him, she takes him by the hand and walks him over to her mother. She smiles at her mother as if to say *sorry*, then she "gives" her father back to her mother. She sees them bonded

54

and happy together while slowly walking away. This retreat makes Kate cry as she experiences feelings of being excluded and isolated (the feelings of losing which are on the flip side of winning). But her soul is reaching for higher ground, where there are no winners or losers.

She moves on to the next person, the 3 year old version of herself. She hugs this person, reclaiming the part of her that is stuck in the past, and they walk together to the next person who is standing for guilt – the guilt of stealing her father and betraying her mother. Looking over at her happy "parents", she sees guilt for what it really is – an illusion designed to keep her stuck in an old win/lose pattern; a trap devised by the mind to squash the soul and thus ensure its own supremacy.

Next she moves to independence. She hugs the person standing for her independent mind, and thanks it for keeping her safe all this time. However, she no longer needs its services, because she is going on to something greater... intimacy.

Intimacy in the "real" world is *physical*, (it conjures up clichéd images of sex, lingerie and candlelit dinners) but intimacy in the energy world is a whole different ball game. It's an alchemical process whereby two energies unite. If an atom consists of a nucleus, around which electrons orbit like baggage on an airport carousel, merged atoms look more like jazz music... with dancing electrons leaping around all over the place.

The space between two people in the "real" world is also *physical*, (one person may be in the office, while the other person is on a train, sending an erotic text message) but space in the energy world is INFINITE. It's an enormous playground that never gets filled up or claustrophobic. And because of this, it contains infinite amounts of erotic charge.

Kate is now shaking as energy pours back into her body. She needs all this new energy to conquer her fear of intimacy, the fear that she will lose herself, merge into nothingness and disappear entirely. This is the moment of truth, when the drop of water is about to fall into the ocean and cease to exist... only to discover a second later "Holy shit, I am the ocean!"

Kate hugs intimacy and turns to face the last person – Tom, who is standing for True Love, minus all the artificial barriers created by the fearful mind. As they walk towards each other there is an amazing, magical, extremely powerful energy in the room.

It is grace.

I'm a romantic. I want to believe that highly charged love can last forever. It's just a question of learning to navigate the "space" better. Learning to manage the energy in that space. My boyfriend had a different view. To him love was an intoxicating cocktail of chemicals that lasted until the fizz went flat. When we were together I made light of his philosophy because I loved the party and I didn't want it to end. We were Scott and Zelda Fitzgerald, bright eyed with champagne, sparks flying from our connected brains, unbound by the conventions of normal life.

But True Love is not how that story ends. It ends with a massive hangover and Zelda confined to a mental institution.

Holy fuck.

Thank God it's the tea break. I carve through the milling people and head straight for the biscuits. The Goddess and Bonkers are already standing in line, one wearing a serene expression, the other clutching a box of herbal tea. "I love that exercise" the Goddess says, "Though it does make me feel a bit envious".

"That's just your ego" Bonkers reaches over to the tea urn "Because we're all connected, Tom and Kate have actually done the exercise for all of us."

"Hurrah. True love is on its way!" The eyes of the Goddess shine with optimism.

"I can hear the sound of horses hooves." I say, grabbing a handful of biscuits, not sure which side of the fence I am currently on.

Beardy man joins us. "So d'you think you could get your man to one of these events".

"Not in a million years" I smile back.

"So what *really* brought you here today?" Bonkers is on to me. I think I've managed to hide the depression quite well, but she's not buying the relationship breakdown. She knows there's a deeper sadness going on. Perhaps she's seeing a vision of a past life, or looking into my Akashic records at some karmic pattern. Part of me thinks this is the answer to a prayer. She can help me find the solution I'm looking for! The other part of me knows this would be just another ego trap... smoke and mirrors to engage my mind in flights of fancy. I don't want wisdom from other realms. It usually means having to join a strange cult where words like Energy vortex, Astral projection and Kundalini rising are NORMAL terms.

I don't want to talk about the depression. I'm grateful to be distracted from it for a day. Half a day if you discount how I felt in the morning. "It's hard to see your own stuff" I mumble. "I'm like Columbo." Blank stares all round as this cultural reference fails to land. "Returning to the scene of the crime for some clue I overlooked before."

"Unconscious stuff" Beardy man nods his head sagely. "Always a fucker. Can come out of nowhere."

"Exactly" I smile back, still grateful for the words "it's not over." Even though, in reality, I know that it is. Over.

Someone once said that "almost" is one of the saddest words there is. "He almost stopped." "She almost made the final cut."

We almost made it.

Sadness rises from the pit of my stomach. I force it back down with a chocolate digestive.

"You can't deal with unconscious stuff through the mind" Bonkers says. "It's trapped in the cells of the body."

"Breath work" suggests the Goddess. "That's the only thing that can release it."

"What rebirthing?" Beardy man looks interested.

I want to run away.

"No, holotropic breathwork " Bonkers continues. It's just a more active way of accessing your soul, if you struggle with meditation.

I struggle with meditation. Well I don't struggle, I gave up the fight a long time ago. My mind is too fast and chaotic. I can't get it to slow down, let alone stop. I can't follow the advice to watch my train of thought, as if watching the closing credits on a movie screen. I have multiple screens, with hundreds of trains, sometimes running side by side, but more often colliding with dramatic effect.

I need breath work. I don't care if I am clutching at straws. I write down the name of the workshop so I can Google it later. The Goddess wants to accompany me. We swop phone numbers and go back into the room for the final session.

There is a Q and A about competition – the particular circumstances that drive us to compete and our individual style of competing – overt competition (masculine) or covert competition (feminine). There are no bad guys in workshops. We're all made of the same stuff, we just have different methods of expressing it.

The final exercise is a timeline. This is an NLP technique in which you imagine yourself hovering above your body, then travelling back through your life along an imaginary timeline. I always find this difficult because of my childhood amnesia, which I have never got to the bottom of.

The facilitator asks us to close our eyes and review in reverse order, all the occasions we have competed – for attention and for love – until we come to the earliest memory.

People who die and come back to life, experience this kind of life review. They say it gives their life new meaning and perspective and they come back to live fuller, happier lives. It helps to have a linear mind when doing the exercise. I close my eyes and a jumble of scenes vie for attention, in no particular order, forward and back. Did I compete with my boyfriend? No, I competed at work, but I was a supportive girlfriend.

How about covertly?

Fuck.

Ok. That will explain why I haven't been able to write anything lately. I wrote for him, so that he would think I was clever, and worthy of his attention. So that he would love me. Now that he's no longer reading, I'm no longer writing. There's no point. He left the competition.

Descartes was wrong... the phrase should be "I compete, therefore I am," not "I think therefore I am."

There must have been a time, somewhere in my life, when the desire to do something came from inside me, like spring water, bubbling up and seeking release. But I can't find one. As my mind scans back and forth, it seems that everything I've done has been a response, a strategy for validation. Far from looking for times and situations in which I competed, I am hard pressed to find a time and situation in which I did not compete, in which I did something purely for the joy of doing it.

I can no longer generate the energy to live my own life, because I am a response to life, not a creator of it.

And now life has stopped giving me something to respond to, there seems no point in anything. A deep, dark feeling of utter meaninglessness begins to overwhelm me.

Einstein was wrong… God *does* play dice with the universe. Stakes have been raised, and I don't even know the rules of this new game.

I just know that I'm not winning it.

As the workshop draws to a close, and I witness the happy, peaceful faces all around me, I feel worse than ever.

NINE

Fumbling Around in the Dark

The nights are the worst part. Being me was always better in the daytime, but when I was younger, I had more to do, so the nights were shorter. Now they're very long and very sleepless.

I review the day's events. It's clear I wasn't the maintenance free girlfriend I thought I was. I had an agenda. One in which I placed some of the responsibility for my self-esteem onto him. No wonder he ran away. I would have run away from me. I am running away from me. I actually don't want to be me anymore.

Woody Allen once said "My one regret in life is that I wasn't born somebody else." I know exactly how he feels.

I don't like myself.

As a rule of thumb, I would not recommend self-help workshops at the end of a relationship, because they make you realize you're responsible for all of it. The good, the bad and the ugly. It's a Molotov cocktail of accountability.

I'm annoyed with myself.

Before the workshop I was dealing with a sense of despair triggered by loss. Now I'm more aware of the reasons I struggled to let go – my boyfriend made me feel like a better version of me. That's why self-help is sometimes called self-improvement. It's easier to love a self that's upgraded, in the same way it's easier to love an iPhone 6 over an iPhone 3.

Self-improvement has now been replaced by the idea of self-love. However, "Love yourself anyway, despite your faults" is a hollow suggestion. It's a nice idea, but it remains just that – an idea that makes no sense. It doesn't matter how much compassion I have for the iPhone 3, how much appreciation I hold for its very existence, it will still be incompatible with the world that surrounds it.

That's my problem. I'm incompatible with the world that surrounds me. As I lie in bed in the dark I am questioning whether there even is a "me" that can be made to feel better.

I don't feel real.

All my life, I've needed people to reflect back to me who I am.

When I look through the filing cabinet of my brain, the only times I have felt really alive, have been times when I am responding to other people. Other people have goals, problems and desires, therefore I create, solve and help. But now I feel detached from life. The only thing I want to be attached to, is not here, and the things that are here I don't want to be attached to.

I am like the drunk man who drops his keys in a dark alleyway, but looks for them under the streetlamp. It's easier to see in the light, but it's a fool's errand, because the keys are not there. Not in the workshop, not in the books, not in the dreams of other people.

But the dreams of another are so much more compelling than a nightmare of your own.

I get out of bed and go downstairs to make hot chocolate. There is nothing to eat. I took a packet of biscuits from the workshop but after eating a few, I threw the rest of the packet in the bin.

Knowing I am lost in a dark sea, the little green light on the computer beckons me, guiding me to safe harbor. It's a lie! It's not a lighthouse, it's a siren, trying to lure me onto the rocks. Soon I am searching social media for signs of his existence. Trying to gain access to a world that is no longer mine.

Stop it!

I close the laptop, go to the bin and retrieve the biscuits. I run them under the tap to remove orange peel and coffee grounds, and stuff them in my mouth. I am a boat that has lost its moorings, desperately trying to anchor myself.

Who am I?

Self-discovery is a lie we got conned by in the sixties. There is no self to discover. Stripped of all the illusions, there is nothing there. I can see who I have been – a daughter, mother, wife, queen, rebel, victim, entrepreneur, damsel, thief – all aspects of a self, not an actual self.

I am a series of Russian dolls.

If the dolls were made by human hand, there would be one exquisitely carved doll in the centre. But God is not restricted by the limitations of time and space, the dolls go on and on, into infinity. There is nothing there. There is everything there.

This is not helping.

I go back to bed to wait for sleep to come.

Einstein said, that in life, there is only one relevant question. "Is the universe friendly?" In other words, it's a given that there is a superior intelligence... we only have to look around for evidence of that. But does it have our best interests at heart? Is it benign presence, or mad dictator?

If it is a benign presence then why the random nature of birth? I could have been born in a country where drought kills crops, insects kill people and male hobbies include rape and beheading. As added evidence of cruelty, the birth rate in these countries is far higher than countries in which a child would have access to clean water, education and the right to say no to someone trying to attack their genitals with a rusty blade.

God seems to play a numbers game. The macro equals the micro. If 300 million sperm are released to fertilize one egg, then it doesn't matter that millions of children live in misery, as long as life can produce one Steve Jobs. That's just evolution. There's collateral damage. But is there compassion? Friendliness?

Perhaps the plot of the Matrix is realistic. If God made everything wonderful, would we strive to evolve? Or would we just hang out and not do very much? We create because we want to make things better. We work hard to get away from bad stuff, and in that striving, discoveries are made, intelligence is increased, the species evolves.

Goals are ephemeral things, horizons that can never be reached. The desire to lose 10k, run 10k or earn $10k, drives us forward but doesn't deliver on its imagined promise. Joy is short lived and necessitates the setting of further goals. Different goals. Higher bars.

I know this but I don't care. I have to hold onto the illusion that goals will make things better, because right now there's nothing else to hold onto. So I sit up in bed and make a list... of all the things I will do, in order to take back control of my life.

I will buy healthy food. I will start juicing, and meditating, and yoga. I will clean out the wardrobe and give things to charity. There are too many books, at least half of them can go. Perhaps colonic irrigation would be a good idea. Put it on the list. Feng Shui will be the order of the day, in both house and body. If I de-clutter the external things, perhaps my mind will give up the fight and follow suit.

Then perhaps, I could finally get... some sleep.

TEN

Negotiating a Way out of Bed

Oh God. I'm awake. I feel as if I've been sleeping under concrete all night. Or maybe I've been awake all night in an alternative universe, one in which I have been extremely busy and productive. I've gone to sleep there and woken up here. No wonder I'm tired. Not just tired, exhausted.

Exhausted doesn't describe how I'm feeling either. That's the problem with depression, it's difficult to describe, just like its opposite – the spiritual experience. Nobody can describe enlightenment. That's why mystics use so many metaphors. There are just no words when you get that high up.

There are also no words when you get this far down. The energy world defies words.

Metaphors and similes act as a bridge between two different realities, for instance heaven and earth. But, like the rickety rope bridges that Harrison Ford crossed in Raiders of the Lost Ark, they are precarious and inadequate. There are lots of casualties in the form of really bad prose.

All the great mystics from Jesus to Rumi have tried to use language to encourage us to cross the divide. "Go through the eye of the needle" must have been a complete mind fuck to a nation of people who had never witnessed the space bending properties of the Tardis, in Doctor Who.

"Unless you become like little children you cannot enter the Kingdom of Heaven" was clearly interpreted very literally by some guitar strumming Christians, rocking their heads merrily to *"Michael row the boat ashore"*. What Jesus meant was that children are curious, creative creatures who live in the present moment. That's the behaviour we need to copy. Adults favor a philosophy that's the complete opposite of this – routine, fear and delayed gratification. But these are the enemies they need to fight, if they are ever to cross the bridge to the promised land.

If Jesus wasn't enlightened, he would have been very, very frustrated at the inadequacy of language, to describe the kind of reality he lived in.

In a similar way, at the other end of the spectrum. there are no words to describe the reality I'm living in. The closest people have got is tired, overwhelmed, sad, raw, valueless, a heavy blanket, a black dog, a forest of gloom. Because these states can be understood in the normal world, many people think they can be resolved by achieving higher goals, for instance becoming successful at something or winning the approval of a peer group.

These same people are momentarily floored when high achieving, successful, well loved people, commit suicide. It doesn't make sense.

Depression doesn't make any sense.

I roll over and pick up the phone. There are no messages, just loads of emails from things I need to unsubscribe from. That should go on the list.

The list.

It's staring up at me from the floor, laughing with derision. What was I thinking? Just getting myself out of bed will be an achievement.

I can do this. Everything is an opportunity. There are no problems, only challenges. The universe is friendly, it's just trying to show me something, teach me something, reflect back some errant belief so it can be transformed.

Transformation.

That's such a lovely word.

The story of Cinderella is embedded in the psyche of every girl. Virtue and self-sacrifice are rewarded with a sequined dress, a prince and a happy ever after. Where did the seed of this story come from? My mother had the Catholic version – the one with added suffering and less sequins. Catholics are high achievers. The meek inheriting not only the earth, but the keys to the kingdom of heaven.

I want transformation, but I want Transformation Lite – the one with the Fairy Godmother and the wand. I'm tired of all this heavy darkness. I need to get out of this bed and out of the house. I will go for a walk in nature. Perhaps, in true Disney fashion, small woodland creatures will come out to greet me and chattering birds will line my path with rose petals, signaling the way ahead, out of the maze, filling me with that magical elixir – the desire to live.

Real transformation of course, is a messy business. When a caterpillar transforms into a butterfly, it goes into a cocoon. (That's a thought. I'm not in a bed, I'm in a cocoon! I'm actually working here!) During the next part of the transformation process, the caterpillar actually melts into goo. It dissolves. But inside the goo are imaginal cells and from these cells, the butterfly forms. The caterpillar literally imagines itself as a butterfly.

The last part is the trickiest bit, when the butterfly has to extricate itself from the hard shell of the cocoon. The effort involved in this struggle enables its wings to form, so that it can fly away. If we feel compassion, we might be inclined to help the struggling butterfly by cutting away part of the cocoon, but this would result in disaster because the wings would not form, and the butterfly would emerge deformed and unable to fly.

So perhaps God *is* compassionate but is more interested in the beauty of my future self rather than the sticky goo of my present dilemma.

I'm surrounded by self-help books, one of them must be able to help. But there's no energy in the books, there's just information, and I already have enough of that in my head.

Coffee.

If I really imagine the exquisite smell, the lovely taste, the feeling of foam on my tongue, I can crawl out of this cocoon and into some yoga pants. Not because I intend to do any yoga, but right now, they're the only trousers that fit. If I get to the piece of carpet outside the bed, there's just one flight of stairs to the cappuccino machine.

I can do this.

After two cups of coffee I take a long hard look at the list. In any journey, several things need to happen. GPS co-ordinates are set, the vehicle is filled with fuel, and the foot placed on the accelerator. My feet work. I have a list of co-ordinates. I just need some DESIRE with which to fuel my will.

Desire is associated with the heart. The mind resists joining forces with the heart, because it wants to reign supreme. The heart likes to give. The mind thinks the heart will give away the store while it's not looking – so the mind does a deal with the body instead.

The body can also create fuel... called adrenalin. Adrenalin is obviously not as good as desire, because it is very limited. Over production of adrenalin can damage the body. Desire on the other hand, being self-generating and sustainable, is limitless.

I've run out of adrenalin.

And I have no desire.

I just need to find something to love. Then desire will come back. Then my life will work again.

Some people are lucky enough to know what they love. They show a natural propensity for things when they are children. They like solving puzzles, or playing with swords or rescuing sick animals. This is when not having a memory of childhood is a drawback. You're surrounded by evidence of skills you have as an adult, but if you're a fairly competent person, there are lots of things you can do as an adult, it doesn't necessarily mean you should make a career out of any of them. It doesn't mean you LOVE them.

And without love, there is no desire.

"Do what you love. Follow your bliss and everything will follow – success, money, meaning." Honestly some self-help advice is just not helpful. I don't know what to love. The things I love get taken away from me by the universe, so that's a clear sign that THEY ARE THE WRONG THINGS. If the universe is benign that is.

If, as Einstein suggests, it is friendly.

"What would you do if you had no fear?"

I don't have any fear.

"What would you do if there was no-one watching?"

Nothing. I would do nothing if there was no-one watching. What would be the point?

I'm not only a sugar addict, I'm a praise junkie. This is going nowhere fast. I will make a pact with my body. We must go for a walk. Stop this endless unhelpful dialogue in my head.

Also if we go out for a walk, we will pass the shop. The shop that sells marshmallows, chocolate covered raisins and flapjacks. Flapjacks are made of oats, which have recently been elevated to superfood status. They also have a sprinkling of pumpkin seeds on top, so Omega 3s as an added bonus. We can easily overlook the fact that they're crammed full of sugar.

Deal negotiated, I finally leave the house.

ELEVEN

Nature that Nurtures

Walking in nature is something self-help books recommend. When you've lost your compass in life, nature can help you get it back. Because nature is awesome.

Being the self-elected vocabulary police of altered realities, I am quite upset that the word *awesome* has been hi-jacked by popular culture. In its original expression awesome had something to do with awe – to be filled with awe. This implies a sacred state of reverence for something beyond comprehension. It's bad enough that we have SO few words to describe the mystical. It's upsetting when they are taken from us and used to describe everything from sit-coms to chocolate cake (though to be fair, in my time I have had some pretty spectacular chocolate cake).

Nature is extraordinary, when we take time out to look at it. But again, the way we look determines our experience. There are levels. Mostly we look on the surface level. This means we see nature as aesthetically pleasing, which it is. Poets have waxed lyrical about golden daffodils, rolling hills and enchanted glades. There is balance in nature. Even untended gardens have a wild, bohemian beauty about them. This beauty is soothing to the soul.

In addition to the aesthetic level, there's the scientific level. Could man have devised something so complex and connected? The mere idea of photosynthesis is mind blowing. Humans breathe in oxygen and breath out carbon dioxide. Trees breathe in carbon dioxide and breathe out oxygen. Leaves take in energy from the sun and convert that energy directly into food. We may not think trees are as intelligent as we are, but when you're in a car on a sunny day, trying to find a parking space at the supermarket, waiting for the opportunity to spend a king's ransom on groceries, just consider... how much more intelligent?

There are many examples of the bizarre nature of nature, but my favorite one is the life cycle of the liver fluke. This creature is so microscopically small, it doesn't even have space for a brain. However, that doesn't stop it coming up with the following survival strategy...

Liver flukes live in the liver of cows and sheep. After mating, their eggs are excreted. The eggs are eaten by ants. They hatch. The baby liver fluke then travels through the gut and takes over control of the ant's brain, forcing it to leave the colony of ants and climb to the top of a tall blade of grass. Once there the ant attaches its mandibles to the grass and waits for a grazing animal to come along and eat it, thus putting the liver fluke back inside the host.

However, if the ant is not eaten by the time the sun comes up, the ant could die in the heat, (killing the liver fluke with it). So in the morning, the liver fluke makes the ant return to the ant colony and act as a NORMAL ant all day, only to repeat its secret rendezvous with the tall grass, night after night until swallowed, releasing the fluke to its livery home.

I mean you couldn't make this up.

So back to the contemplation of nature. We have the artistic perception of nature (beauty and harmony) and the scientific perception (wow, really clever) but there is another deeper perception which, for want of a better word, you could call sacred. This is the perception of the shaman. The shaman occupies the space between the two and the space, is ALWAYS the best place to inhabit, because it's alive with infinite intelligence.

In the new-age where there is a huge market for Spiritual Lite, a shaman is someone who spends his weekends beating a drum, chanting and guiding people on vision quests. He's smart enough to know the different properties of plants so he can mix up healing brews for the kind of ailments that modern doctors can't treat.

For an investment of a few thousand dollars and a few weekends in the woods you too can become a shaman. Except not really. This is just marketing.

The reality is quite different.

A shaman is someone who has transformed his consciousness to such an extent that he can tap into the different (not better, not worse, just different) consciousness that is inherent in plants.

I suppose this is a little bit like Horse Whisperers. First they have to tone down the dial on their human consciousness (otherwise the horse will not play ball). Next they tune into the consciousness of the horse. Then they are able to occupy the space between them. All communication happens in this space.

Lots of animals perceive on a much broader bandwidth than humans. Dogs hear sound frequencies that are inaudible to our ears. Birds see three times better than we do. Dolphins send messages to each other across vast expanses of ocean. Bears can detect the smell of a dead animal from 20 miles away. Many animals can sense tsunamis and earthquakes days before they happen.

When we developed a neo-cortex, we became so enamored with the upgraded functions of our new brain, that we lost the skills of the old one. Now we place quite a high mystical value on these old skills. We think it would be really cool to sniff the air and sense "a change in the force", like Darth Vader or Neo in the Matrix. It is possible to do this, but very few people are prepared to put in the necessary hours of discipline.

The idea that plants have consciousness is a ridiculous concept to humans, because we are only interested in our own perceptual system. But scientists now have proof that plants do have consciousness. In order to access this consciousness, the shamans of old would go into the forest and live like a hermit, eating only the leaves or roots of one plant for several weeks at a time. In this way they came to "know" the plant in an intense, intimate way.

Intimacy is a true merging with "the other" – whether that "other" is a plant, a person, or a deity. We argue and fight over the OBJECT of our attention – particularly if it's a deity – but it's the PROCESS OF MERGING that's important. We're back with triangulation. There's us, there's the object (plant/person/deity) and the space between. Intimacy involves meeting "the other" in that space. It doesn't look like much is going on in the real world because it all happens in the energy world.

This is what the shamans do with the plants. It's what the mystics do with God/Jesus/Shiva/Buddha/Allah, and (apparently) what tantric sex practitioners do with each other. The alchemical process of union, allows them to go through the narrow gate to higher states of consciousness.

I am in the park now, sitting on a bench looking at a bunch of trees, wondering how Tom and Kate are getting on. Will their intimate breakthrough last? Is it already over? The mind hates intimacy, because it loves individuality. It thinks that if it merges with "the other" it will lose its identity and die. That's because the mind can't cope with paradox, so it always has to pick a side.

For instance if we are light (something Einstein would agree with) then we are made up of ALL the colours of the rainbow, which mixed together come out as white light. Within this magnificent spectrum, the mind chooses to think it is red. The mind ALWAYS has preferences because that's how it establishes individuality. If blue comes along, it backs away. However if it moved towards blue, in an intimate embrace, it would make PURPLE. Not only is purple a great new colour but it also includes both red and blue. It is the new thing and it is the two individual things at the same time.

My boyfriend preferred the colour black. It's long been the cool elegant choice to wear on the outside. I now feel black on the inside, which of course is not so attractive.

So back to the shamans, on their own in the middle of the night, battling inner and outer demons – the cold, the loneliness, the mosquitos, the craving for a mug of hot chocolate. I'm sure there are many shamans who thought they would die on the third week of their strange diet. I'm struggling to add kale to my lunch, so the thought of JUST kale for three weeks is really hard core. It's certainly not for Spiritual Lite people.

But at the end of three weeks you could say that the shaman was pretty intimate with the kale, to the extent that the kale starts to share some of its different kind of intelligence with the shaman. Basically the kale needs to know that you're serious about the relationship. It doesn't give up its properties for pussies.

The ritual that many shamans are associated with is the Ayahuasca ceremony, in which consciousness raising hallucinogenic plants break down the rigid barriers of the ego mind, allowing a glimpse into the alternate realities that lie behind. The ingredient that enables this mystical journey is DMT. DMT is completely inactive if consumed alone because there's an enzyme in our gastro intestinal system that breaks it down.

However! The Amazonian shamans overcame this problem by boiling up the Ayahuasca vine together with the Chacruna plant, which shuts down the enzyme, thus allowing the DMT to go through the gut into the bloodstream.

So consider the lonely shamans sitting in the jungle, surrounded by THOUSANDS of different species of plants. I mean they're still discovering them. This is bio diversity central. Yet despite the odds stacked against them they find the ONE PLANT that allows this incredible alchemy to take place. Without technology or microscopes. Without laboratories and a Big Pharma research budget.

"How?" you may ask. "How did they know?" And the shamans reply...

"The plants told us."

Different intelligence. Different approach. We may think we are smart. But despite our superior intellect, we still haven't found the cure for cancer. Perhaps we're directing our questions in the wrong direction.

The park is full of life. I watch a variety of happy people go by. Oldies walking their dogs. Lovers walking hand in hand. Kids on bikes. Why can't I be happy with simple things? Why do I feel hell bent on destruction? My own destruction.

All these people in the park seem to have the desire to do things. They're living in harmony. I stare at the landscape in front of me, trying to connect to the slow rhythm of life, instead of the chaotic discord of my mind. There is creation and destruction. Plants die, become compost and rise again the following year. It's a circle of life, slow and graceful. I'm the one who's out of step. I'm angular and stuck, unable to move forward, no option to go back. I need to create, but my dial is jammed. I'm blocked.

If I could slow my brain, I could increase my skills of perception. Hear beyond the shouts of the children, to the sounds of tiny mice building their nests in the undergrowth. See beyond the branches swaying in the breeze, to the photosynthesis occurring in their leaves.

I sit on the bench and become as still as I can, taking slow deep breaths, observing the wonders of nature. Trees, brightly coloured rhododendrons, long strands of ivy, beds of nettles. None of them are talking to me. But if I need their help, I should probably get more serious about it.

An Ayahuasca Ceremony? The idea scares me, but I feel a psychic frisson as the inevitability of a future event tries to reveal itself.

One day.

Maybe.

"Cos maybe...
You're gonna be the one that saves me..."

TWELVE

Red Red Wine

Oh God I'm awake. You might notice a theme. The repetition serves to illustrate that this is the way I wake up every day for about three months. I won't describe each morning. You can now take it as a given that morning is always a really bad time.

Today, however is much worse than yesterday. I'm not just tired, my body actually hurts, like I've been in some kind of celestial boxing match with someone or something that's trying to kill me. My bed is no longer a safe cocoon, it is Mad Max's cage in the desert. Not even the thought of coffee can get me to stand up.

I imagine the people who love me, ring-side coaches with water bottles, soft towels and shouts of encouragement. *You can do it. Just one more round.* I can't do it. I scan my body from head to toe. There isn't an ounce of energy anywhere. I'm in a hospital bed, surrounded by anxious people. I know I am letting them down, but I just need one more shot of morphine. I fall back into a semi conscious state, trying to remember the previous day.

In an attempt to overcome my insomnia I had drunk wine.

This may not sound like the worst idea in the world. Wine, being made from grapes, is wholesome so it isn't "bad" alcohol. Absinthe is more commonly associated with artistic madness and Tequila is just a euphemism for a full-blown death wish, but wine conjures pictures of sociability – afternoon picnics and convivial dinners.

I rarely get drunk. I was saved from this particular form of addiction by a fear of dizziness, which I've had all my life. As a child, I hated swings and roundabouts. Other children were delighted to jump on and off moving things. But when I tried to join them I would be reduced to white knuckled terror, gripping the nearest solid thing, as I tried to stop the tarmac rising and falling.

Control. I always have to be in control. I don't like things that move when they should be stationary. It's why I would struggle with an Ayahuasca experience. It is impossible to control.

Learned behaviours are great short-term strategies. A "need for control," translates easily into "attention to detail," something that the world values quite highly. And during my life – my previous life, the one I had before the madness of this depression – I was valued. I look back on that life now with a kind of envy.

No challenges, opportunities. No mistakes, lessons. What was life teaching me? That my old life was unsustainable? That my mind was an obsolete computer that needed to go for recycling? That it was time for my soul to take over? No wonder I'm fighting. Apart from an abstract, vaguely poetic notion, I have no idea who my soul is or what it wants to achieve here.

Whilst sitting in nature the previous day, trying to be still, trying to silence the noise in my head, I didn't hear anything from my soul. Perhaps I don't have one. This thought is my mind's absurd contribution to the debate – the melodrama of specialness. The whole world has a soul... but not me. Mine has been gambled away in some Faustian pact. I know this isn't true. It's just that my mind is stronger because it's rigid with control. Unlike the branches dancing in the wind, it refuses to bend and sway. That's why it has to be broken or rendered unconscious by a sharp blow.

Or a bottle of wine.

That's what happened. The wine. It's made everything so much worse. There must be some other way to contact my soul. If I can't find it in nature, perhaps I can find it in church.

I haven't been to church since I was a child. I threw out religion as soon as my mind switched up a gear. Religion went in the charity box with all the other stuff I'd grown out of – sandals with T-bars, Ladybird books, Easter bunnies. I was a precocious teenager and loved to argue with religious leaders about the concept of metaphor.

"He wasn't the biological son of God. God doesn't have a penis. It means there's a bit of divinity in all of us. It's just that Jesus actually realized his divinity and we haven't."

As a word of caution, I'd advise against discussing God's genitals with members of the clergy. Their replies usually include reference to "an immaculate conception." There are numerous works of art that depict this Annunciation event. None of them give as much as a token nod to the biological component. They certainly don't show the angel Gabriel carrying the wriggling spermatozoa of the Almighty in a glass vial.

Because it's a metaphor.

The energy of God impregnates us all. We are God in potential. But that potential remains a seed, undeveloped, dormant. Even the vegetation in the park knows how to grow itself into what it's supposed to be. What's so messed up about humans? Why can't we develop into higher conscious, divine, creative beings?

Because we have a mind.

Maybe God thought it was time for a species upgrade. Maybe it was Christmas and we asked for one, so that we could create new, better, more complex things. (Good idea!). But now the mind is out of control, creating mayhem and madness.

Sadhguru says that the mind is a useful tool, in the same way a garbage bin in the kitchen is a useful tool. But you wouldn't want to live in the garbage bin. If you're a mystic, this is what it feels like to live inside the mind – as opposed to having a mind that you use whenever required. Being an adaptable species, we can learn to live in garbage. But the divine seed inside us, knows that something isn't quite right. It knows that if it can just get access to some light and air, it will grow, flourish and escape the confines of its metal tomb.

Take me to church.

THIRTEEN

The Divine Feminine

I don't agree with religion. But I remember the peace inside those heavy stone walls. You don't get that feeling in modern churches.

The pagans who came before the Christians lived in harmony with the energy world. Just like the acupuncturists who, thousands of years ago, figured out the energy system of the body, the pagans figured out the energy system of the land. They built their devotional sites on energetic ley lines.

The early Christians had a bit of a dilemma on their hands. They had a new religion to sell. Their manifesto had some pretty tricky bullet points – like no sex before marriage, babies being born with original sin, deities being born to virgins. Plus lots of other rules, all written down in a large book called (without a trace of irony) the Good News.

You have to bear in mind that at this point pagans celebrated life, so sex (which is a precursor to life) was therefore thought to be a good thing and women, who gave birth to life, were an even better thing. Women were loved and respected, not subjugated. Far from being blackened with original sin, babies were gifts, that came like spring lambs and summer flowers to bring joy and beauty to an abundant world.

How did the Christians, with their unpopular rules, achieve this take over bid?

In the same way that right wing governments, who only look after the interests of a wealthy minority, can get elected... by creating fear.

In the case of the Christians, this was Fear of Women. In the good book, women were clearly Bad News. The first woman (Eve) brought all the pain and suffering into the world by disobeying God and encouraging Adam to eat an apple from the Tree of Knowledge. Obviously God didn't think humans were ready for the upgraded brain software contained in that apple.

If so, he had a point.

The undisputable evidence that women were bad was re-inforced by the fact that the new God had absolutely no feminine aspect. This was the WILDEST idea of all. Everything has a masculine and feminine element – people, animals, plants, the electrical cables that make your television work. But not the Christian God... God the Father, God the Son and God the Holy Spirit are ALL male.

We can see already how our world got completely out of balance.

However, going back to the energy, the Christians knew they had to pull a rabbit out of a hat, so they built their churches ON TOP OF the pagan sites. This kept everyone happy. The Christians felt the powerful energy, which they could attribute to the efficacy of their prayers, and the pagans could carry on as normal, but with the added benefit of a roof.

I am now outside the heavy wooden door of an old church. There are gravestones to left and right, an almost quaint custom now that cremation is the preferred option. I used to love reading gravestones,

"Not dead, fleeping!" I would try to determine the cause of death from the age carved on the stone (Something hideous like the plague, or something simple like a sore throat, before the discovery of antibiotics).

The door is not locked and I walk inside. The smell of damp stone and decaying lilies greets me. I sit in a pew at the back. There is one woman walking around the stations of the cross. Her footsteps echo but that's the only sound.

Being educated in a convent I miss the ambience of the church. I love the silence when they're empty, the thick stone blocking out any external noise. I love the sound of the organ when they're full, the congregation hesitating, just off the beat. I love the visual splendor of high arches, fat pillars and stained glass. The woman completes her vigil and the door creaks open as she leaves.

It's like the inside of a tomb. I get up and walk to the statue of Jesus, hanging on a crucifix above the altar. How could the teachings of such an exquisite man be so crassly interpreted? How could he forgive people, even as they were knocking the nails in his feet, splintering the bones, hoisting him up, to hang naked while slowly suffocating. How could such humanity and such inhumanity co-exist in the same place?

But then I look at the tableau below to witness another kind of suffering – that of the women. His mother and Mary Magdalene. Suffering is bad, but watching someone you love suffer is worse. Because the suffering isn't in your body, it's in your mind. And long after the physical suffering has ended, it goes on and on and on. These women were living at a high frequency, where the feminine has the power to contain energy in order to transform it. It's a really tough gig – note there were no men at the foot of the cross.

After the crucifixion Mary Magdalene went to France, where she is honoured and revered as a spiritual leader. There she carried on teaching the philosophy of Jesus – which was LOVE. Unconditional love. The Catholic church of course tried to shut her down. There was no money in this kind of love – the love that brought its own reward. They preferred a more masculine approach – transactional love. This included competitive killing (God will reward you if you destroy his enemies) and competitive bartering (20 gold coins and this fingernail of St Joseph will guarantee you a place in heaven).

For hundreds of years the two philosophies operated side by side. The feminine, more esoteric, teaching adopted by the Cathars and the masculine, rule based teaching of the Catholics. As the Catholic church grew in power, however, it got meaner and nastier (that's the thing about masculine energy which remains unchecked). The Catholics upped their game and came up with genocide, the inquisition and the mass burning of all Cathars.

While the world was becoming more masculinized and the feminine was becoming demonized, there was the slight problem of how to write Mary Magdalene out of the story. They couldn't get rid of her because wherever Jesus was, she was with him. So they came up with the ingenious idea of turning her into a reformed prostitute.

Much later, the Vatican apologized for this fiction, but of course the apology was on page 7 of the Catholic Herald, so the old story prevails to this day. Clearly the media were as powerful then as they are now. More powerful because there was no social media to "out" them.

It wasn't just Catholics that denigrated the feminine of course. Most western religions interpreted the "word" of God through a very distorted masculine perspective. Women's creativity, sensuality and sexuality were all squashed. Women couldn't enrich the world with their creative gifts; couldn't balance it with their sensuality; couldn't express their sexuality unless they were "owned" by a man. And that was hardly an act of expression, more one of duty. They could have sex if they produced sons, and of course as long as they didn't enjoy it – hence the need for genital mutilation.

There's a strong argument to suggest that most of the problems we are currently experiencing (war, political corruption, corporate greed) have been caused by our disconnection from feminine energy.

Right now, I have no energy at all, either masculine or feminine. I don't have the will to do anything or the heart to love anything. My only joy comes from the thought of the hot chocolate I'm going to buy as soon as I leave the church. Perhaps with an added shot of brandy to help with the hangover, and the shock... of realising that my life has absolutely no direction.

I've forgotten to bring a handkerchief, which is awkward as tears are running down my cheeks and out of my nose. I have to wipe them on my sleeves. I'm a mess. My mind is broken and my soul still hasn't made itself heard. Everything feels impossible, both inside my body and in the outside world.

As I stand in front of the crucifixion scene, I wonder if we will ever learn. Learn to overcome our fear filled, judgmental, competitive minds. Learn how to love. Not love as we know it – self-serving, sentimental and narcissistic. Love as they knew it – transcendent, intimate and divine.

Because I have a feeling, that this love would be the ultimate cure for depression.

FOURTEEN

Resistance to the Life Force

"Live in the Now" is the kind of new-age advice given to depressed people. It implies that the thing that caused your depression happened in the past. Therefore if you leave the past behind, you can successfully leave the depression behind.

Reading the accounts of other people, one common theme keeps emerging – although the depression was often triggered by an event, the event was definitely not the cause of it. The event was the crack, the opportunity for what was underneath to surface.

As Einstein pointed out, we can't solve our problems with the same level of thinking that created them. We usually interpret Albert's advice as the need to go to a higher level, but this rarely works, because we're a pattern. We need to go down to fix the pattern, not hover above it in a positive spin.

One of the few memories I have of my mother, is the one in which she is knitting. Most women used to knit, particularly in working class towns, where the arrival of evening wasn't marked by the sound of cicadas but by the click clack of needles. I can see now that this pastime wasn't just practical (nobody could afford shop bought sweaters) but it was an ancient ritual that calmed the mind. Women didn't sit in meditation, listening to the chants of Tibetan monks, they sat behind half a dozen kids, ignoring the sounds coming from the television... knitting.

When I was old enough to be introduced to this ritual, I struggled to make the perfect square. It's difficult to keep the tension consistent between soft wool and hard steel. And of course, it's easy to drop a stitch and not be aware of it until AGES later when there is a hole in the middle of the square. It's REALLY frustrating, but the only way of fixing this problem is to unravel all the wool and go back to pick up the missing stitch.

There are three possible responses to this.

1 Rise above the frustration and JUST DO IT.

2 Accept (but be constantly irritated by) the damaged square.

3 Throw the thing away and NEVER KNIT AGAIN.

Being a rebel, my preferred option to the trials of life is normally Number 3. But now that I'm struggling with depression, I can't contemplate the third option, which would be to "throw life away and decide never to live again."

I also can't contemplate the second option – accepting the constant irritation of a life without any energy, full of scary black holes. So the only option left is to go back to the place where things went wrong with the pattern. Not in my lifetime. But in our collective lifetime – the one we share as a species.

If depression is a loss of connection to the life force, then why, as a species, are we becoming more and more disconnected? If life is one interconnected whole, what creates a rogue cell?

On a physical level, scientists still don't know why cells go rogue and create (for example) the pattern of cancer, but there is a correlation between cancer and a body that's out of balance.

On a holistic level, the world is dangerously out of balance. We presume that our early ancestors lived in harmony with life, but this was before the patriarchy was established. That's when we dropped the stitch and the imbalance between masculine and feminine energies began.

In some parts of the world this imbalance is being rectified, but in other parts, it's still the dark ages. Mostly there's a grey area in the middle where there's change on the surface (female CEO's) but same old story underneath the surface (female CEOs with massive amounts of masculine energy). It's what goes on in the energy world that really counts. This has nothing to do with gender.

We need to find and embody the missing feminine energy if we want to restore balance to ourselves. But first we have to establish what exactly that is.

There's a lot of talk these days about "being in touch with your feminine side." This generally implies men paying attention to the more subtle things in life – they don't cut their hair, they style it; they don't barbecue burgers, they lightly sear tuna; they choose taupe not turquoise. They even know what taupe is.

But the feminine isn't subtle. It's something so powerful that men tried to kill it (death by burning). When they couldn't kill it, they tried to control it (second class citizen status, just slightly above that of slaves). And when they couldn't control it, they tried to bribe it (Be like us and we'll let you into our inner circle! Swop those worthless magic beans for this lovely cash cow).

I admit, I succumbed to bribery. At one point in my life, I didn't even want to hang out with women, in case I accidentally caught the virus of vulnerability. Like a desperate Catholic believing in the power of St Joseph's fingernail, I bought into the whole myth – that masculine power was strong and the only power worth having. But this is ALL propaganda. Masculine energy without feminine energy to balance it, becomes really dysfunctional. It looks good on the surface, but underneath it's a train smash.

We haven't even seen a functioning representation of balanced power yet. Culture and the media generate stereotypes of feminine energy – earth mothers, sex kittens, wispy waifs, ditsy dames, camp men. While we're obsessed with these identities, we'll be very reluctant to show up in life and play our part. After all, who wants to play a cliché?

We need a new definition for feminine energy.

Perhaps it's something about the space between things... containing the energy within that space, so it can be expressed creatively.

On a literal level, this can mean interpreting the space between objects. After all, a good website is one where the designer has contained the impulse to fill up all available space with as much content as possible. It's the relationship between each of the elements and the space between them that creates something that is aesthetically pleasing, and therefore much more functional.

Most people laughed at Steve Jobs when he brought this same concept to product design. Now they all copy him. This is him, sounding exactly like a mystic...

"Simple can be harder than complex: You have to work hard to get your thinking clean to make it simple. But it's worth it in the end because once you get there, you can move mountains."

(Steve knew all about the mustard seeds. And the magic beans.)

On an energetic level, the feminine can mean mastering the space between people. If we walk into an office meeting, everyone *looks* normal and the conversation *sounds* good. But in the space between them is all the unwanted energy that allows them to retain this cool exterior – all the resentments, jealousies, and fears. And of course all the competition.

Meetings often feature highly intelligent people with really good ideas so it's disappointing that so few of these ideas become a reality. It's the energy that drives the ideas that's important. And if this energy between colleagues contains repressed emotions, the resulting pattern looks messy and full of holes. On the surface, everyone is on the same page. Under the surface, everyone has their own private agenda.

At the inspirational level, the feminine is about co-creating with life, because space contains infinite possibility. Life is a force. This means trusting that whatever comes will be handled in the moment, rather than hiding behind old strategies and insurance policies.

We can't protect ourselves from bad stuff, but by defending against it, we block good stuff from happening – opportunities, chance meetings, serendipities. These all happen in the present moment, and can easily be missed when we're busy looking back at the data or checking the future for possible problems.

Living in the now is... actually living.

Depression feels like being in resistance to this feminine force. We can feel this as profound sadness (the sadness of a soul that wants to create, but is blocked). We can feel it as madness (the futile attempt to process infinite amounts of data – welcome to the digital age). We can feel it as numbness (the inability to feel anything at all – how I feel most days).

We are supposed to co-create with the energy of life.

Developing an intellect gave us the ability to do this. But we quickly forgot about the "CO" in co-create, which is a very small word for a very big deal. Masculine energy ran away with the idea of INDIVIDUAL creativity. They created things – castles, bridges, trains. They created concepts – currency, capitalism, christianity. They created movements – the renaissance, the industrial age, the technology revolution.

All good, but without the "co" things have got out of hand. Whole species are being eradicated – whales the size of buildings die from ingesting plastic sheeting, unsuspecting birds feed their infants with brightly coloured bottle tops, thousands of species of trees, fungi and insects (any one of which may contain the cure for diseases we haven't encountered yet) are destroyed so that McDonalds can create more burgers.

And we think none of this affects us on a cellular level?! It's a wonder we aren't all depressed.

There is a war going on between the individual and the collective. Between one person's quality of life and the whole quality of life. Between the individual's desire for convenience, and the inconvenient truth.

Co-creation enables us to make choices that not only enhance the experience of the individual, but simultaneously enhance the experience of the whole. This doesn't make sense to a mind that believes only in winners and losers.

But there is another intelligence in the universe. Intelligence that is bigger and better, that copes easily with complexity and paradox. All we have to do is co-create with this and we'll solve all our problems and be able to create amazing things without the terrible side effects.

This intelligence is sometimes referred to as God, but in reality it's far too big for a name. In the field of creativity, the higher you go up the ranks, the shorter the names become. For instance people like Madonna, Cher and Sting don't need a second name.

God doesn't even need a first one (though as a clue, the force is sometimes referred to as THE creator).

The portal to this creative state of consciousness is through the right hemisphere of the brain, often referred to as the feminine side (which of course we thought had no value). Most education systems focus on developing the left hemisphere of the brain, which deals with logical thinking and calculations. This is quite sad because we now have computers to do all that stuff, and meanwhile the world is crying out for creativity.

"We are all made in the image of God" means we all have the capacity to create. It's an energy that comes through us. Saying "I'm not creative" is like a tree saying "I can't photosynthesize". You're a tree, you have leaves, and you're in the sun. It's going to happen.

However humans have free will. Which means we can close ourselves off to the creative force and refuse to contain it. I know I've done this. Not consciously. Nobody wants to be depressed consciously. But a part of me has thrown a spanner in the works to stop the energy coming in.

Depression is the curse of the creative mind, but paradoxically, creativity might just be its cure.

FIFTEEN

Is the Universe Friend or Foe?

I have decided to disregard my old list of things to do and goals to achieve and replace it with a new strategy of engaging in creative pursuits. I'm going to start drawing.

If depression is resistance to the energy of the life force, then I need to find a way to be a better conduit for it. If I can get SOME energy to move through me, then perhaps this will blast the dark energy out of my system. This image is a bit masculine, but reconnecting with your feminine side doesn't happen overnight.

I don't know why I didn't think of this before. As a coach, this is what I would have recommended to a client, but depression has a funny way of messing with your mental faculties. Or, as one of my best friends would say "Here, take my advice – I'm not using it."

I am still finding it impossible to write, apart from incoherent journal pages, so decide to take a walk up to the shops to buy new pencils, a drawing pad and a large bar of chocolate (it's dark and organic so this counts as health food). I manage to resist ripping open the chocolate until AFTER I get home, make a pot of tea and sit down. This is a major result.

The white page is instantly intimidating. I don't have a grand enough idea to justify such lovely cartridge paper, so put it to one side and grab some cheap photocopy paper instead. This gesture implies that my inner world is rubbish and unworthy of decent materials, but I let that one go for now. It's important to do baby steps at this stage in the recovery process.

The new pencils fill me with nostalgic joy. There is something wonderful about pristine stationery, that reminds me of a new term at school. A fresh start, filled with the resolution to keep on top of things, complete course work and not leave everything till the last minute.

Beginnings contain all that wonderful hope and optimism.

I was educated in a convent. It was the only place you could get a good education that was also free. Nuns didn't earn money and lived very frugally. Their job was to turn Catholic girls into Catholic women. We all came out emotionally dysfunctional but with extraordinary talents in conjugating French verbs, the correct positioning of an apostrophe and the ability to endure humiliation without crying.

One thing I did love about being a Catholic was confession. There was, of course, the pre-confession fear of whether the priest would recognize your voice. Then the awkwardness of saying things out loud – the kind of things that fought to remain inside your head. But afterwards... oh the bliss! Your mind wiped clean. Ready for new beginnings. A fresh start.

These days I suppose therapy is supposed to serve the same purpose. But it doesn't. You say things, so that gets them out of your head, and you pay a huge amount of money. But you don't get any divine enema blasting through your system. Therapy is a fairly masculine approach to depression. The idea is to change the pattern by gaining a different perspective and a new strategy. But connecting the dots, isn't the same as connecting to the source of life.

My mind wouldn't allow me to stay a Catholic. But I miss the grace. I just need to find a different way to access it.

The life force, aka God, doesn't need us to follow the rules, and rituals of religion, these were invented by men who love politics and costume parties. But the discipline they required, did serve a purpose. Praying creates an altered state in the person doing the praying. This state allows access to higher levels of consciousness.

These days, many people connect to God through nature, art, poetry, sex, or random acts of kindness. However, some things remain the same. God doesn't require our prayers, we do – because we need a way to make the mind quiet, before the spiritual realm can make itself known to us. It doesn't matter what the method is. It just matters that we have a method.

Drawing is a good form of meditation, and luckily it's one that doesn't involve buying into any crazy belief system. If I can't write, I'll draw. One hour every day. The same time every day. This will be my discipline, my signal to the divine, the flare that goes up announcing "I'm here. I'm in the space. Come and meet me." This is probably a better prayer than my original thought, "I'm lost. I need help. Get me out of here."

In general mystics don't recommend making demands of the divine, because we can't see the whole picture. We can't understand the complexity of what's really going on. Depression might be a Cosmic Time Out, in which we are stopped from creating further destruction. God could be putting us on hold, while a fleet of angels in the Genius Bar sort out the mess we've made of our hard drive. If so, I might as well draw instead of sulking in the corner.

I find a really good playlist on the iPod – Velvet Underground, Massive Attack, Amanda Jenssen and Erykah Badu. If I am in a waiting period, at least I can curate the on hold music.

There are random items on the desk – coffee mugs, books, pots of pens, screwed up pieces of paper, headache tablets, chocolate wrappers, a half finished glass of wine. Perhaps I should draw everything on the desk – my version of Tracey Emin's bed. An homage to a life that stopped working. Or perhaps I could do a Damien Hurst – just encapsulate the whole thing in Perspex and call it "Writer's Block".

In the same way that my mind flits from one thought to the next, my eye flits from one object to the next wondering where to start. This is a good way of making a connection between subject and object. Between me, and the stuff on the desk. The pencil will navigate the space between. The pencil becomes the end point of a funnel – infinite random thoughts at the open end of the funnel, single point of focus at the other.

I like this form of meditation. After an hour I feel better. More peaceful. I'm pleased I didn't use the expensive paper because I am now surrounded by a massive amount of cross hatching. Perhaps I'm ready to start writing again. I pull up an article I've been working on, but still no words come out in any meaningful way, so I mess around on Facebook instead. His page has no updates that would provide any insight into his world.

Stop stalking. Now. Just stop it. Let go. He's becoming another addiction.

A friend has been diagnosed with an illness and is being super positive about it. I feel guilty all of a sudden. I have no illness. I should feel happy and grateful for my physical health. I'm beating myself up again and have to remember the mantra...

Depression is not logical.

New-age people believe that illness follows the same trajectory as creativity does – from external to internal. Idea to form. Energy to matter. Once the illness is in the body it can be observed on an MRI scan. This is the hospital drama scene where doctor and patient stare at the solitary grainy photograph. But what if the camera had a fast continuous shutter and there were hundreds of photographs? In the midst of this, there would be two images – one where there was nothing there, and one where there was something there. What happened in that single frame?

A thought?

A thought that created an impulse in a death direction instead of a life direction?

This implies that some part of our mind says "yes" or "no" to the illness that's about to arrive. It's bad enough having people think that depression is something you choose, but it's cruel to suggest that cancer is something you want to create.

"Not consciously of course" the new age people rush to say. I wonder how the Goddess from the workshop would deal with a major illness, or Beardy Man, or Bonkers woman. I suppose that's why they work so hard to stay healthy. They don't know how they would fare if they were tested – would they increase their meditation practice, or go straight for the hard drugs?

If illness is a rogue thought, that creates a pattern, that later becomes a big mess further on down the line, then how did that original thought begin?

Going back to Einstein's big question (is the universe friendly?), there are two possibilities.

1 There is an external **unfriendly** force, that can take over our brain (in the same way the liver fluke takes over the brain of the ant, causing it to climb to the top of the blade of grass to commit suicide). Perhaps this is the experience of people who jump off the Brooklyn Bridge. A kind of temporary insanity.

2 There is an external **friendly** force, that is trying to teach us better ways of living together in harmony and love. When this

force starts to connect with us, our independent mind locks the door to keep it out, thus creating a siege. Starved of love, the soul finds ways to engineer its own suicide, either quick and dramatic (bungee jumping without the rope) or slow (morphine assisted terminal illness). The soul, being an eternal being has no fear of death. Death signals the end of one life and the beginning of another. In a sense this is a bit like the choice between walking out of the movie half way through, or sticking it out to the end in the hope that it gets better.

Increasing our consciousness – by becoming more conscious of our thoughts – seems to be the way we are heading in terms of evolution. Hundreds of "mindfulness" programs have sprung up, to help us do this.

As the speed of life increases, so do the consequences of our decisions. We invade Iraq, we create ISIS. We take the fat out of food, we create obese people. We administer antibiotics, we create superbugs. Now, more than ever, we need to connect to a higher form of intelligence. Otherwise we'll keep on making really stupid decisions.

There is currently an epidemic of depression in the western world, with one in ten people on anti depressant medication. (In some areas, and some demographics, the figure is one in four). Each year the number of prescriptions rises to stratospheric new levels. Children are depressed (Why?) Rich, successful people are depressed (WTF?).

We have lost our connection to the whole, and without this, we're a bunch of disparate individuals who are messing up what could be a brilliant, creative future. People who identify with God as masculine energy, say God is really angry with the mess we've created. "He" wants to punish us. This is why we're having so much crazy weather, tidal waves and earthquakes.

But the feminine energy of God isn't cruel, or something to be frightened of. "She" realizes we dropped a stitch or two. But if we're willing to be unravelled, we can be knit back together again.

I'm certainly unravelling.

But perhaps this is a good thing.

I'm quite comforted by this thought because it gives meaning to my current predicament. Suffering is bad, but suffering for no purpose is worse. I am being re-engineered, in order to become a better container for the energy. This means a positive future.

Where are we going as a species? If we could time travel, what would our future selves look like? Probably as different as we are to the Neanderthals. We can reason, see two sides and make intelligent decisions. Perhaps our future selves will be able to read the energy, see ALL sides and make inspired decisions.

The word "inspired" comes from "in spirit", meaning you're listening to the energy not the data. Data is often wrong. Data can easily be manipulated. Data is associated with the mind. The spirit, on the other hand, is associated with the truth.

And the truth, of course, sets us free.

SIXTEEN

What's Love Got to Do With it?

A week has passed and I'm starting to feel better. The daily drawing practice and walking in nature are working. Writing is still impossible, because I can't seem to hold on to any of my thoughts long enough to get them down. They've become as fleeting as dreams. Thoughts come, but when I open the laptop they dissolve or become really convoluted. This is a strange sensation because my mind has always been the one thing I could rely on. I'm half out of my mind. But currently, it's not unpleasant, it's just frustrating. I have to be grateful for this small mercy.

Because of the "drawing meditation" success, I've come back to the church, to try "proper meditating". I'm not making much progress, but I'm determined to crack it. All the books say that meditation is the key to physical well being and a peaceful mind. In the beginning, of course, it's a bit of a catch 22 – you want to meditate to get a calm mind, but you need a calm mind in order to meditate.

There's another catch. If I AM being unravelled, in order to be re-fashioned into a lovely piece of knitting without the holes, my childish mind is going to fight this process, and I do sense a looming identity crisis. In the "real" world, an identity crisis announces itself with the arrival of a sports car, a younger wife or an extreme sport. It can also involve cosmetic surgery, cookery courses in Tuscany or an extreme eating disorder. As in everything, there's a masculine and feminine element.

In the energy world, an identity crisis is like a Mexican stand off between the mind, the heart, the body and the soul. The mind wants to stay the same, the heart wants to do something meaningful, the body wants to stay young forever and the soul... we have no idea what the soul wants, but it has something to do with co-creativity.

Who am I?

I only know what I turned myself into – a rebel. I refused to acknowledge the damsel because she didn't fit with the personality I'd created. Because we create our personality, we feel compelled to defend it, in the same way we defend all our creative endeavors (*It's called an HOMAGE... you just don't understand. Philistine!*)

Anything we TRULY are, we don't have to defend. It's our essence. It defies comparison. It laughs at performance metrics. It doesn't answer to any valuation system. This essence is underneath the personality we have created.

So what's the problem?

There's something in between the two – a HUGE fear that the mind fashions to act as a sentry to the soul. This is why we can't experience who we really are. I thought this was the damsel. But the damsel is just another personality, the flip side of the rebel. She's annoying but she's not frightening.

The mind is really clever, so when it wants to create an effective fear, it doesn't come up with something generic like fear of spiders, it makes something bespoke. Lately I've realized what mine is.

My greatest fear is that I'm boring.

I kept my distance from the "good" girls at school. The ones who were obedient, handed their homework in on time, and never took risks. I would rather die than be like that. The kick ass rebel personality I created was a reaction to the fear of being boring, and now that its been knocked sideways by the depression, we've come face to face.

I'm boring.

This is hideous, and little wonder that I want to distract myself at every opportunity.

Why is there never any chocolate in the fridge? Don't answer that.

My instinct is to fight it by becoming the opposite version of boring. But this is a masculine strategy...

"Create goals! Interesting ones! Get drunk on a school night! Do outrageous things! Wear strange clothes! Listen to music that no-one else understands!"

Masculine strategies no longer work. I can't run from anything in the energy world, it's always there. I have to learn to love this part of me. That's the only way to transform anything. Love the one who has no ideas, no creativity, no value to offer the world. Love the one who's not cool.

Oh God, this is impossible. How can I love her?

I have to remind myself that the independent mind has endless strategies to keep me trapped and separate from life. These include creating faulty beliefs – peace is boring; surrender is dangerous; love is a battlefield.

I look around the church for inspiration. There's a statue of Francis of Assisi here – another mystic who succeeded in breaking the dictatorship of the independent mind and connecting to the realm of higher consciousness. I imagine his mind resembles a Star Wars inter galactic council containing monks, humans, angels and large furry creatures, all of whom have a voice and a chance to be heard without judgment.

I can't help thinking that becoming enlightened might have been easier in the 13th century. The pace of life was slower, the distractions were fewer, and addictive substances were less easy to get hold of. There were no vending machines in sleepy medieval towns. No corner shops offering 50 types of confectionery. No gauntlet to run on the way to church.

St Francis is associated with nature and is usually portrayed surrounded by animals. He had inner peace. This seems to make you a magnet for non-human species. Inner peace allows you to join a tribe of gorillas, like Jane Goodall or become a horse whisperer, like Robert Redford. If Francis had been born in Peru, instead of Italy, he'd probably have been a shaman.

The other advantage of living in the 13th century, when it comes to spiritual surrender is the culture of obedience that prevailed. Children did as they were told. Obedient children grew into dutiful adults. Independence wasn't a popular concept. Acceptance into the tribe was – whether that tribe was a family, a church or a guild of stone-masons.

It's a different story now. We celebrate disobedience. Naughty children are called "spirited". Rebellious children are called "unconventional". Free thinking children are called "creative". This is great, up to a point. These attributes gave me the capacity to thrive in a competitive world.

Independence gave me immunity from rejection by the tribe. But independence is a curse if you're trying to get through a dark night of the soul, because that demands surrender and trust.

It's hard to surrender. Looking over at Christ hanging on the cross, I'm reminded of the way he put it. "Thy will" not "my will". This is not someone who was pitting his will against the wishes of his father. It was a metaphor for surrendering his association with the physical world, in order to align with a higher dimension.

It takes trust.

Like most independent people, I have very little trust. If I really want something doing, I can't ask for help. I can only delegate things I "sort of" want. That way I can avoid feeling disappointed.

There was a large framed picture in the assembly hall of the school I attended. The same picture was in the houses of many of my Catholic friends. It was Jesus pointing to his heart – only his heart was on the OUTSIDE of his clothes. It was called The Sacred Heart. I just thought it was really strange.

Now that I'm familiarizing myself with the world of symbols, I have a different interpretation. The re-engineered human needs a new heart. A heart that is capable of being a container for the energy. A sacred heart.

A heart that is turned inside out.

St Francis has a very famous prayer, *"Lord make me an instrument of thy peace."* In typical mystic fashion, it reverses everything – it turns them inside out.

"Lord... Grant that I may not so much seek
to be consoled as to console;
to be understood, as to understand;
to be loved as to love;
for it is in giving that we receive."

111

This kind of love makes no sense in a competitive world, because our kind of love is based on an exchange of value. If I give, I need something back BECAUSE THAT'S FAIR. If I put up with your dysfunctional behaviour, you should put up with mine. If I love you, you should love me back.

We like to own the things we love, whether these things are iPhones or boyfriends. We also like to control, so we put things in writing (a sure sign of no trust). We take out an insurance policy on the iPhone and we want our spouse to sign a contract that they will love us for ever. But love is an energy, not a thing. It can't be corralled, locked up or guaranteed in any time and place other than the present moment.

The only truthful marriage vow would be "I love you in this present moment, and I hope our life will continue to be a series of moments just like these".

Shakespeare wrote a lot about human love. When love turns to hate – (*Othello*). And when hate turns to love (*Much Ado About Nothing*). They show how fragile our version of love is. The thought that his wife is unfaithful is enough to turn Othello from lover to murderer. Just one thought has the power to do this! Except it's not just a thought, it's a thought coupled with an emotion (jealousy).

In *Much Ado*, Benedick and Beatrice start off hating each other, until their friends come up with a cunning plan. They tell Beatrice that Benedick is secretly crazy about her and they tell Benedick that Beatrice is secretly crazy about him. Just the thought, coupled with an emotion (I am loved!) is enough to completely turn things around. As far as romantic comedy is concerned, this basic plotline (from "I can't stand that guy" to OMG he's amazing') hasn't changed much in 400 years.

But there is a different kind of love – the one St Francis was talking about. A love that can contain and transcend emotions. Commitment to this kind of love brings absolute freedom.

There are a lot of women currently looking to experience this kind of love with a soul mate. I was one of them. My boyfriend. (Am I still hanging on by a thread to Beardy man's prophetic statement "it's not over?") My *ex* boyfriend was a bit of a doubting Thomas. "Look around you" he'd say. "Married couples are pretending. Either they secretly hate each other, or they're just friends pretending that the passion is still there.

I was determined to prove him wrong. If I'd come up with the proof, maybe he'd have understood, and been curious enough to go there with me. I definitely needed the St Francis prayer. I was seeking to get understanding and love, instead of giving them unconditionally.

I knew my life wasn't working before this darkness descended on me. I was looking for love in all the wrong places. In a boyfriend. In a chocolate bar. In a writing career. I'm wiser now. And with this realization, I feel the faint stirrings of optimism. I felt them earlier while I was drawing, but didn't want to jinx things with premature hope. But it must be true, that discipline is a signal to the divine. Help is on its way. I can feel it already.

Optimism is now blending with excitement. If I'm at level one, I can easily get to level two. After all, the first step is the most difficult. I'm ready to make a plan... a strategy for a better life. One that will involve meditation, yoga, and a diet of green things. No animals (I'm sure Francis of Assisi didn't eat his friends). No artificial food (evil corporations are the enemy). And definitely no alcohol (that's just the wrong kind of spirit). Starting now, because there's no time like the present. (Actually there is no time, there is only the present – something both scientists and mystics can agree on).

I stand up from the pew, give St Francis a nod and walk back for the last time to the crucifixion scene. When I used to look at this image, it made me imagine what intense physical pain would feel like, but now my eyes are drawn to Magdalene. To bear mental anguish and emotional pain with such grace...

That's a container.

That's what it means to be an instrument of the divine.

An instrument of the peace.

I don't want to get better so that I can go back to my old life. I want to be reverse engineered so that I can live in a new one.

As I leave the church, I'm actually smiling.

SEVENTEEN

This is Madness

What. The. Fuck. Happened.

How can I go to bed happy and wake up like this? My improved condition was a cruel joke, because now I'm back at square one. I've had no alcohol for a week. Something strange is definitely going on during the night. "Be careful what you wish for" is a phrase that's bandied around these days. It's supposed to mean that you have to prepare yourself for things like winning the lottery, in case you subsequently lose the money.

But I wanted access to spiritual things. Like St Francis, I wanted to be connected to the life force. My inept spirit obviously made a wrong turn during the night, because the only part of life I feel connected to, is something dark and floundering, like a sea bird covered in oil.

There is a fairytale I remember about an old shoemaker. His eye sight was failing and he was exhausted and there was some life or death situation that necessitated the making of shoes. He went to bed distraught and woke up to find little elves had made all the shoes for him.

I'm living this story in reverse. I went to bed happy, having succeeded in knitting myself back together, but malevolent sprites came in the night and unravelled it all. Now I'm lying in a tangled spaghetti of dark thoughts while my chest is in a vice of fear.

I can't even find peace under the duvet. Waves of emotion make me feel like crying for no reason. I get up and try to keep to my routine, but drawing is impossible. I feel claustrophobic and need to get out of the house. Perhaps I could draw in the museum. I've seen other people do this, perched in front of marble statues, absorbed in lines and curves. They look peaceful.

I want to feel like them.

Picking up my sketch pad and coat, I head off to the train station. Half an hour later I realize what a bad idea this is. I'm deep in the bowels of Waterloo underground feeling nauseous and dizzy which, for me, is the worst feeling in the world. I need to change lines, but my head has turned into the large hadron collider. Thoughts aren't running around, they're pinging at lightning speed. My body is trying to cry but there isn't even enough energy to do that, because all the energy is in my head.

I lean against the wall and try to breathe calmly. There's pressure behind my eyes and beads of sweat on my forehead. People are rushing past to get on the train, and this constant movement just increases the nausea.

This isn't the kind of depression I'm familiar with. It feels like madness, like I'm dissolving internally into goo. Why is this happening here? I should be in bed. That would be safer. Perhaps my imaginal cells are running riot because they don't know how to re-form. Sweat is now pouring down my back. I close my eyes to shield myself from the chaos of people, but this makes me feel dizzier, which is worse.

I just need to get on the train and go four stops. Four stops then up an escalator and I'll be in the quiet calm of the museum. But there's a loose wire in my brain that is making me want to do the opposite thing. When the train doors open I feel pinned to the tiled wall by some centrifugal force. When the train leaves I feel a strange urge to rush forwards onto the track.

Freud wrote something about death wishes. But Freud is impossible to read, so I don't know if he revealed how to overcome them. Neuroscience says there's a part of the brain (the hippocampus) that acts as an internal sat nav. Mine seems to have developed a fault and is sending out all the wrong signals to the rest of my body.

I don't trust myself. I can hear a train coming and I have to close my eyes and imagine myself clinging to the white tiles of the wall, because there's nothing to hold onto. I can't board the train. I need to ask for help. Find someone. Pretend to be blind. Don't tell them I'm going crazy. People aren't scared of physical things. Someone will help.

People rush from the train to the exit. Their eyes are focused straight ahead, no peripheral vision, and they walk too quickly for me to stop them. Very slowly, I unpeel myself from the wall, edge backwards towards the escalator and leave the station.

This is definitely madness.

Things are getting worse not better. I sit on a bench looking over the river and eventually my breathing returns to normal and the panic is over. I don't want to move for the foreseeable future so this is a good time to regroup and figure out what's going on.

1   I asked for this. I distinctly remember asking for more connection to the life force.

2   The life force is not all unicorns and rainbows. That's just new age marketing. If there's light, there's dark. If there are angelic forces, there must be demonic ones. Not at the higher frequency, but I certainly don't live there yet.

3 Being a container for the energy is great if you're hanging out with St Francis, Jesus and Mary Magdalene, but not so great if your high voltage friends aren't around.

4 Demonic is just an identity. Energy doesn't have intention. Tornadoes have a lot of energy but they're not evil. That's just fiction for people who like gothic stories.

5 Maybe I'm the one with the malevolent intentions. *Shit*. But that's only a part of me – Bat Shit Crazy Girl with a death wish. Hiding right behind Boring Girl. How clever, she knew I'd NEVER look there.

6 Love is the answer to everything. How many more parts of me do I have to love? Crazy Girl. Boring Girl. Judgmental Girl. Inadequate Girl. Greedy Girl. There's a boat load of asylum seekers in my brain.

I wonder if the people in the workshops have figured out a way to deal with unconscious urges. Do they have special spells and incantations? Perhaps they reframe it into an *Alice in Wonderland* experience? "Oops must have stepped through the looking glass, while gazing at my reflection." I was pretty sure the Goddess and Bonkers woman were pretending with their version of spirituality. But how would I know?

I need to stop being so cynical. If we're all connected, then forgiving them for their version of Spiritual Lite will bring forgiveness for my own brand of fraudulent behaviour – pretending to be a cool person who has it all together. That's quite funny given my present circumstances. If my ex boyfriend could see me now, he'd definitely run a mile in the opposite direction.

This feels better. We're all a little bit mad really. I start thinking kindly about the people in the workshop, and wonder if the Goddess has found her soul mate and Bonkers has found a way to earn a living channeling advice from extra terrestrials. I've noticed a lot of stuff on the internet lately about the Pleiadians. Now that the baby boomers from the US military are retiring, they're coming clean about their interactions with a number of off planet species. They have nothing to lose (they're approaching death) and they have a mass communication tool at their fingertips.

Bonkers is not bonkers after all. She's just slightly ahead of her time. One day in the future, we'll look back at ourselves, in the way that we look at our ancestors. They believed the world was flat. We believe that within a hundred billion galaxies, we are the only intelligent life. What's even more hilarious, is that we believe we ARE intelligent.

And Beardy man! I wish I'd taken his phone number. I could do with some Gandalf style reassurance right now. Particularly as I seem to have just taken a visit to Middle Earth.

Two teenage boys walk past in very hip skateboarding gear. I wonder if they've ever been on a skateboard. If not I forgive them as well. Flipping a skateboard looks easy but it's actually extremely difficult to do and takes months of practice. It's reasonable to assume that surfing the life force requires even greater amounts of practice. I smile at the boys. Who am I to judge? I thought I could reverse decades of competitive, self-centered thinking, with a couple of church visits and a reasonable likeness of Michelangelo's David.

I feel calm watching people wander up and down the bank of the river. There is a completely different rhythm of life here. The polar opposite to what's going on below ground. People smile and walk slowly. Perhaps the water is the calming influence, or perhaps we weren't designed to thrive below ground. It could be the association with too many metaphors... Hell, dungeons, the dark tunnels of rats, dragons and escaped convicts.

Eventually I get up and make my way home. As I pass the shops, the craving begins... followed quickly by the justification. I've had a nasty shock. People suffering from shock are always given sugar.

Besides, I need to go to the supermarket to buy the green things in readiness for tomorrow. That's when I'll begin the new regime.

Crossing the threshold, I realize that this is my real church. I walk in a trance like reverie towards the chapel of confectionary. This thought causes me to remember my first communion. The excitement of direct communication with God! Opening my mouth to receive the little wafer, being so careful not to let it touch my teeth. You can't chew the body of Christ – that would be disrespectful. You have to let him melt on your tongue, while divine grace floods your body, pouring compassion into all the hurt parts, hiding in all the difficult to reach places.

"God's love will always find you" the nuns used to say. "If you pray hard enough."

I've ripped open the packet of chocolate now and place one square on my tongue. I chew immediately of course. I might let the fourth square melt, or the fifth. The sensation of sugar rushing through my veins is calming. But it doesn't heal. It isn't God's love, it's the corporate counterfeit. The sham high. The false Idol. Already I feel weak and ashamed with my body, so I pull the focus back up to my mind.

Women are programmed by evolution to look for bright colours. While cave men were out tracking wild animals, cave women searched for coloured berries in the forest. Corporations exploit this genetic tendency by making the packaging as appealing as possible. We're practically trained, biologically, to ignore the leafy green background and reach for the soft, pink marshmallows.

Now that I've had a sugar fix, I can focus on the actual shopping. But by the time I reach the fresh food section, all the vegetables, look dull and uninviting. I buy them anyway. Salad. Broccoli. Kale. Avocados. Pumpkin seeds. I'm determined to do this properly.

On the other hand, because I'm starting the diet tomorrow, I might as well eat today all the things I will never be able to eat again. I put cake and ice cream in the trolley. I don't want to leave anything out because THIS IS THE LAST DAY.

My old body is on death row, so I need to devise the absolutely perfect last meal of sweet delight. Tomorrow I am going to go to war against the corporations who make these foods. They may look like normal people, but they are in fact the devil. They whisper things that sound rational "Oh we're just providing variety. Don't blame the food, blame the consumer".

In their obsession for profit, corporations are like drug pushers at the school gate. The phrase "Give me the child and he's mine for life" was first uttered by a Catholic Jesuit missionary, but like all good principles, it's been exploited by the dark side. The Jesuits were trying to engineer a stairway to heaven, while the corporations... they're just busy paving a highway to hell.

EIGHTEEN

Dealing with Emotions

I go home and start writing in my journal, about the strange experience on the underground. I can't draw madness, though Edvard Munch did a reasonable job in his picture *The Scream*, so I'll write instead – while eating ice cream and cake.

"God's love will always find you…
if you pray hard enough."

God doesn't seem to hear or speak through the inadequate communication device of words, which is why so many prayers don't work. God exists in the energy realm. What would be the energetic counterpart to this piece of advice?

God's love will always find you…
if you hold still and stop moving about?

This makes more sense. If our spirit is a beacon of light, it isn't helpful to have that light whizzing around in and out of the body like a firework that's gone out of control. Prayers can be rattled off in parrot fashion, but it takes discipline to keep the spirit still.

When thoughts and emotions are negative or crazy, the spirit tends to leave. The spirit is made of energy. It can walk through walls, so it's not going to be deterred by a layer of skin.

The love can't find us. Because we're not there.

That's why the modern equivalent of prayer is meditation – keeping the spirit in the body while the thoughts and emotions compete for air space. This makes the soul more resilient, which makes it a stronger container for the spirit, so the spirit is less likely to leave when the going gets tough.

In the childish world, prayers are requests we make to God – *I don't like what's here, please change it for something better. Here's a list of things I think would be MUCH better, just so you know... because I'm not sure I trust your choices.* This presumes God is a bit like Father Christmas.

In the energy world, prayers are intentions (less about what we want to have, more about what we want to be). *I want to be happy! I want to be connected. I want to be creative so that I can make life better myself.* These are still "I want" prayers, instead of "I am" prayers. "I want" has an energy of neediness, "I am" has an energy of gratitude. The universe amplifies what we feel, so gratitude prayers tend to be more effective.

As a rule of thumb, if we don't get the answers we seek, we're usually asking the wrong questions. Instead of asking to be connected to the life force, I should have asked a better question, like...

How can I become a better container for the energy?
How can I manage energy better?

Emotions are energy in motion. I'm really bad at managing emotions as they happen... in the present moment. I always put them away so I can go through them later when no-ones around. When it's "visiting time" I alternate between good cop/bad cop. Sometimes I bully myself "You seriously screwed up. You should be ashamed of yourself. Idiot." Sometimes I'm nice "You were just feeling insecure, don't feel bad. Here, I brought cake."

Going over emotions after the event doesn't work, because by then we're safely back in our mind, while the emotions are trapped in the cells of our body. Analyzing doesn't release them, it reinforces them.

Most of us don't know how to process emotion in the present moment, because we don't LIVE in the present moment. We live in a world of thought. All thoughts are either imagination (the future) or memory (the past). We can't have a thought about the present moment – by the time we have a thought about it, it's already in the past.

A life lived in the mind is a life of imagination and memory. It's no wonder we feel as if there's something missing – WE are the thing that's missing. And the more our body gets filled with trapped emotions, the more missing we become. Perhaps that's why we love smart phones. They allow us to live in a virtual world, far away from what's going on inside us. Life is pleasant in a virtual world, but it's not real. We may be barricaded from pain, but we are also cut off from joy, love and bliss.

As far as emotions go, we all agree to abide by the following rule NEVER SAY HOW YOU FEEL. For example...

At work a boss criticizes an employee. The employee feels humiliated and disrespected. He seeks the company of others who feel the same way, portraying the boss as the villain while they are the victims. This gives them a great excuse for all kinds of dysfunctional behaviour – blaming others, calling in sick, stealing the stationery. The boss feels wronged. How can he be a good leader when nobody respects him? In his mind, the employees are the villains and he is the victim. He gets defensive and keeps looking for further evidence of their villainy.

Multiply this by thousands of employees and you can see that a lot of energy is getting wasted on things that are NOT GETTING THE JOB DONE. Of course you can't PROVE any of this because most of it is going on in the energy world. In the real world, everyone is being nice and polite to each other. The employee can't say anything because he doesn't want to risk losing his job. The boss can't say anything in case the employee summons the services of a tribunal, which HR say will cost the company a fortune. Nobody says anything but EVERYONE IS ANGRY.

In personal relationships it's advisable not to have ANY negative emotions – particularly neediness, jealousy or anger. We feel them of course, but we replace them with an image constructed from a thousand media sources of "how to be in a relationship" – which is cool, confident and unattached.

Love stories are often more about power, than love. Boy meets girl. Girl isn't that bothered. Boy becomes crazy about girl, but pretends to be cool and charming. They fall in love. Boy loses interest. Girl feels heartbroken but pretends to be chilled and patient.

This "feeling one thing while doing another" is also rife in other aspects of life, like buying a house... Find a house. Fall in love with it. Pretend it's not that great, point out all the flaws, and be slow to return phone calls. After all, if the seller knows how much you love it, they won't do a good deal on the price.

We become practiced at masking our true feelings. It may save us money in the real world, but there's a price to pay in the energy one. We become disconnected from our heart and we're sitting on a minefield of repressed emotions.

When the "me" that I'd constructed collapsed, I was faced with all the emotions I'd buried along the way. I don't have a portrait in the attic, I have one in the basement.

I'm going to do a 180 and confront all these repressed emotions. Perhaps in this way I can get them out of my body. Open the gates and release the prisoners. Where to start? I write down a list of emotions. The first one that catches my eye is betrayal.

When was I betrayed?

I remember a work situation. A team of us were working on a product launch. We weren't just colleagues, we were friends... until something screwed up. One of the guys blamed me for the error behind my back. I don't remember the emotion of betrayal, just the shock, and the immediate rush to find a defence strategy while remaining cool.

Work is a masculine environment so it was inappropriate for me to feel what I was feeling in the moment – probably a combination of tears, injustice, anger, and betrayal. Instead, my mind said something like "Incoming. Impact imminent. Engage shock absorbers". All the energy went straight to my head, leaving an unexploded bomb in my body... while my mind got busy fantasizing about revenge.

I need to love the Betrayed Girl.

And I probably also need to love the Vigilante Girl.

How many more asylum seekers are there? I definitely need God's love, I haven't got enough to go round.

So if that's the betrayed, the next question must be...

When was I the betrayer?

Ugh!

It's so much easier to feel anger than it is to feel guilt – something the Catholics used to their full advantage. I betrayed my ex boyfriend by looking at his emails. Whenever I think this thought, my stomach twists and I feel self hatred. I pride myself on respecting other people's privacy. But pride comes before a fall, and all my lofty principles turned to dust in front of the open laptop.

I want a giant eraser to rub out the memory.

When we do stuff we're not proud of, we go straight to our head because it's REALLY uncomfortable in our body, and because the mind is great at coming up with rational excuses to justify the behaviour. "You were feeling vulnerable and insecure. It's understandable."

When we behave badly, other people say "It's fine, no big deal, I've let it go." But often, this isn't true. We've been trained to process data, not energy. We're not skilled at letting things go, we're skilled at ARCHIVING them.

Much later on when the relationship has ended, we say "love died slowly". But it didn't. It died in an instant. All it took was one thought. One emotion. One stitch that got dropped... leading to the creation of a very different pattern...

Not in love.

A thought seems like such an insubstantial thing, yet it has SO MUCH power. If we knew how powerful our thoughts were, we wouldn't get out of bed. Maybe that's why I can't get out of bed in the morning. I've discovered who I really am – a terrorist walking around with a suicide belt of bad thoughts. This idea is really depressing.

The radio has become a boring drone, so I put on some music to cheer myself up. This doesn't have the desired effect. The iPod shuffle has chosen Lou Reed, which brings back happy memories, now transformed into sad ones by his absence.

Just a perfect day, you made me forget myself.

My mind is cruel, unforgiving and attacks me relentlessly. I'm not disciplined enough, not creative enough. I haven't done the things on the list, haven't written the book. I can't even manage to eat a normal diet, or get on an underground train.

He made me forget myself.

The impossible bliss of that achievement.

The peace within that space.

I decide to have a hot bath and an early night. Sleep before midnight is better apparently. It's more virtuous than sleep after midnight. Maybe I'll avoid the night demons who lurk on the edges of sleep in the wee small hours (that means one or two o'clock right?). It's 10pm. Ten is a big number. Sleep at ten o'clock is guaranteed to be carefree and peaceful.

I light some candles and put lavender oil in the water. Perhaps a glass of wine will perfect this sleep inducing ritual. After all, today is the last day I will drink alcohol so I'd better take advantage of it while I can. There is no wine, but there's a bottle of gin. There's also no tonic so I add some coconut water – now it's virtually a health drink.

Submerged in the fragrant steam I realize I forgot to eat any dinner so the gin takes effect quite quickly. It strikes me that this is what Victorian women did to induce abortion of unwanted children. Perhaps in a similar fashion, I can expel my unwanted inner demons. Gin and hot water. What a genius idea. I don't know why I didn't think of this before.

NINETEEN

I Heard the News Today, Oh Boy

I know why I didn't think of it before! Gin is a ridiculous idea. No wonder it's called Mother's ruin. Staggering down to the kitchen to get a drink of water, I do feel ruined. This is not a good day to start a health regime. All the optimism is missing. I make coffee, but without the sweet vanilla syrup, it's just not doing anything for me. I'll have to start the diet tomorrow, when I don't have a hangover.

That means I can throw a coat over my pajamas and go to the café for a chocolate croissant. Feelings of failure start to kick in, so I quickly reframe the situation. I am not a sugar junkie, I am an artist living in France during the 1930s. Cafés, croissants and mad thinking are all quite NORMAL.

Context is everything.

A few minutes later I'm desperate to leave the café. This is a bad sign, because the café is one of my safe places. I love the aroma of the coffee, the reassuring whir of the milk frothing machine, the lovely array of cakes in the glass cabinet. But the café has been taken over lately by mothers and buggies. This really annoys me. Particularly given the strange new way mothers speak to their offspring – a fusion of kindergarten teacher, university professor and Old Mother Hubbard.

I heard one of these exchanges the other day, in the park, while I was trying to contemplate nature. A nasally toddler said "Are we going all round the park mummy?" and she replied "Yes Noah, it's called a perimeter. Now hurry up darling and we'll have time for a babycinno before we go home." There are just too many words wrong with this sentence.

With the invasion of the mothers, it's hard to reframe my experience. There were no children in Parisian cafes in the 1930s. At least not in my mind, which is the only place reality exists. It isn't warm enough to walk in the park, so I decide to have a wander around the supermarket instead.

Pretty soon I am staring into space completely confused. My heart is racing and I have difficulty breathing. I know tears are coming because I can feel them being squeezed from the tightness in my chest. I leave the trolley in the middle of the aisle and rush out of the shop. There's a bench near the entrance and I sit down and allow the tears to pour down my face. Luckily nobody notices. Customers are used to people in this spot, rattling tins for charity. They are conditioned not to make eye contact.

I am going insane.

I have no control over my mind anymore. When I need to do something practical, it won't engage. When I want peace, it runs riot. I should phone somebody. Let them know how I'm feeling, but I don't want to talk, especially about how I'm feeling. I want to escape. But of course every place I go, the thing I'm trying to escape from is still there. This is a strange kind of torture.

I go home and put the radio on. Other people's voices will distract me from my own inner voice. The presenters are discussing *Tiswas*, a Saturday morning kids show from the late 1970s. People are phoning in with their nostalgic recollections. One caller told of his excitement at being part of the live audience. Thousands of children wrote in, so being picked was a bit like winning the lottery. He was in the front row, and was drenched with a bucket of water during one of the sketches. Far from recounting this experience as one of shock and humiliation – he had reframed it into a badge of honour that said "I was there!" The event was proof of his participation.

We're always trying to prove something because most of the time we're missing from our lives. But there's a deeper problem caused by our not being present.

We don't feel real.

We need intense experiences, not just because we have a "fear of missing out" but because they provide evidence that we exist. That's the problem with living in the mind, instead of the body – everything feels hazy and unreal. The mind creates the opposite of an embodied experience. Embodied experiences create joy, whereas the mind can only create hope, nostalgia or regret.

Memory and imagination.

These days, instead of carving our initials on a tree, we have thousands of selfies. Constant reminders of our existence. Many people think this is the result of the narcissistic times we live in. Hello magazine screams "Look at me!" (in my fabulous home, with my fabulous children, at my fabulous wedding). "Look at *more* of me!" (in my low cut dress, side slit dress, totally transparent dress with strategically placed sequins).

Self-help books say that our constant need for validation results from low self-esteem. It's a problem of the mind... "I don't feel worthy; I don't feel good enough; I don't feel loved."

But maybe that's rubbish. Maybe it's a problem of the soul... "I don't feel like I'm really here."

I don't feel like I'm really here.

I turn off the radio and watch the news on my computer. It's bad. Over a thousand refugees have drowned on rickety boats, trying to get from Syria to Italy. Hundreds more drown trying to escape Myanmar. The survivors are huddled on the shoreline. Mothers are crying, looking frantically for their children. Fathers, glassy eyed, just stare into the distance, defeated. They have been unable to do the one basic thing that would give meaning to their life – the ability to provide for their family.

Journalists speak to interpreters trying to capture the worst (and therefore best) stories. These people have been deceived by traffickers. Their life savings have been given to unscrupulous profiteers. They have lost all their money, their loved ones and their last chance of any kind of life.

One man made the trip to look for his 12 year old son who went missing the previous month. Children are sold into the sex trade so are given free places. It's easy to lure them away from a life of hardship. A can of coke and the chance to play football will just about do it. The father of the 12 year old had already paid the ransom money to get his son back. But the traffickers lied. His life savings gone, the father borrowed money to pay for his own passage. Now he was kettled in a pen, waiting to be sent back. No hope of repaying the money lenders. No son. No peace from a mind full of the imagined horrors his son was experiencing. No sanctuary from a heart torn with the pain of being unable to protect his child.

This is a hideous world. The universe is not friendly. It's evil, cruel and unfair.

After world news, there's coverage of the upcoming election. Polls show growing popularity for the party promising to deal harshly with immigration. All problems are blamed on migrant workers.

There is an epidemic of fear and a call to close the borders before we are over run with foreigners. One spokeswoman referred to them as cockroaches. I wondered if she could look into the eyes of the father whose child was missing, and feel no pity. This noble man, who had just made the most perilous journey in the world, on the slim chance that he could save his child, was being referred to as vermin.

I turn off the news and try to distract myself on Facebook. There are always mindless bits of clickbait and cute videos of cats. Not today. I open the first video on the news feed. It's the story of Kulwa Lusana, a young African woman with albinism. It's not uncommon in parts of Africa. She speaks through a translator. When she was a young child she was not able to go to school. Having no protective melanin, and being unable to afford sunscreen, she would easily get sunstroke or skin cancer. Every day she had to stay in the house doing the chores, washing, cooking. She would prepare her siblings' school uniform each evening, but was unable to join them.

It's a sad story. An accident of birth. But it gets worse. There is a lot of superstition in Africa and a belief that albino body parts can be turned by witch doctors into powerful potions – spells to attract love or money. It's just like the Catholics in the middle ages with their relics made from the bones of saints. One night while Kulwa was sleeping, five men rushed into her bedroom and hacked off her arm. She said the pain was indescribable, but she was saved by a charity that took her to a safe house and taught her to knit. The final minute of the video shows Kulwa with a shy smile, proudly showing the jumpers she had knitted with her one arm. She missed her family but she was grateful to be alive and to have the means to feed herself.

I can't breathe. My throat is tight and my neck feels weak as if it can't support my head anymore, so I lie down in a fetal position and cry. There's nothing else I can do. I don't have a plan. There is no strategy.

I'm not grateful to be alive. I'm angry and powerless and drowning in a tsunami of emotions. I don't know how to live in this world. I don't even know if I want to.

TWENTY

The Breathing Workshop

The Goddess calls. At first I have no idea who it is, then I remember the workshop. Talking feels strange. It's been a week since the incident on the underground and I've hardly spoken to anyone during that time. This means I've only been listening to the voices in my head, and those voices are increasingly vicious.

My anxiety is at an all time high. Sometimes I don't even know what I'm anxious about, there's just this discordant vibration in my body, as if the world is running on one frequency and I'm running on a different one. I'm worried about money, worried about work, worried about the refugees. Mainly I feel like a complete failure.

I walk around the park in a trance, wishing I could have my old self back. The one that could just do things. The one that wasn't paralysed by self doubt. I try to draw, but criticize the results, and hate the lack of talent they reveal. I want to be good at something.

Not good, better than good… perfect. I think this would take the shame away. The shame of being me.

I know this reveals my dysfunctional belief system. I've read the books. I know achievement won't remove the pain of imperfection, but my beliefs are too entrenched. I don't know how to love the things I don't like, particularly when one of those things is me. Needless to say I didn't start the health regime. When you don't feel like living, you certainly don't see the point in steaming up a load of broccoli.

One of the upsides of being a writer is that it enables you to hide quite successfully. Nobody comments on the fact that you haven't shown up for work, because you work at home. If you do speak to somebody and say you're still in your pajamas at noon, they think you're lucky to be able to have a "dress down" day. There's no need to mention that this dress code has entered its second week, and nothing has been written yet.

"It's Jane! Sorry I haven't been in touch. Soooooo busy. It's been crazy around here. I said I'd let you know about the Breathing workshop."

"I've been pretty crazy myself." (Jane doesn't pick up on the irony of this statement).

"So d'you fancy coming with me? I know it's short notice, but it's going to be soooooo great. Some friends of mine went last time and they're still raving about it."

I'm about to decline the offer but a small voice takes advantage of this gap in conversation and I suddenly find myself agreeing to meet her. I put the phone down. What was I thinking? I can't manage to buy vegetables. I have to leave the café if a yummy mummy enters. How will I be able sit in a room full of chakra healers and crystal activators.

On the other hand, crazy people may be just what I need to feel normal.

I have two days to remember how to dress myself.

I hate walking into a room full of people at the best of times. I think many of us do, it's just that we've perfected our own ways of making it feel normal. Some people are friendly – big smile, ready to make the eye contact necessary to start a conversation. Some people are shy. Some people look for things to do.

Everything is energy, and energy moves in three ways – forwards, backwards, or against whatever it comes in contact with. We are energy, so we enter a room in the same three ways.

We advance. *I love your sweater!*
We retreat. *I'll just sit by the door in case I need to leave.*
We engage. *Must check my emails, update my status, fiddle with my fitbit.*

Because I'm contrary I don't have a preferred option. If I'm in a room full of shy or hostile people, I will be sunshine personified, breaking ice and connecting everyone together. However this being a workshop, all the uber positive slots are already taken, so I can feel myself withdrawing, a few seconds after entering the room. Thought is fast. One thought is powerful and can affect the trajectory of the entire day.

Everyone sits in a circle and introduces themselves. There's a bald headed man in his forties. He was a roadie in a rock and roll band but is now a personal trainer, looking to expand his skills. There's a small mousy woman of similar age who's a school teacher. She's been in sacrifice her whole life and is on a journey to become empowered. There's a round faced, smiling woman. I have no idea why she's here because she doesn't speak in actual sentences, just hokey aphorisms... as if she's just swallowed The Little Book of Calm.

There's a very tired looking woman who's trying to heal from an abusive relationship, and a young blonde one who's an astrologer. There's the Goddess (Jane) whose eyes glow with mutual bonding whenever the astrologer speaks. Sisterhood yay! Introductions complete, we lie down on the floor, the facilitator puts on music and we start to take really deep breaths.

This kind of breathing releases emotions that are trapped in the cells of the body. I like the idea of it because it doesn't involve the mind, and the mind is somewhere I'm trying to escape from. When we experience a strong emotion, not only does our focus shoot straight to our mind, we also momentarily stop breathing. Fear makes us hold our breath. This is what traps the emotion – it's effectively vacuum packed in the body, so it has a very long shelf life. Breathing (if it is deep and consistent enough) can "pop" the sealed unit and release its energy. Some people remember the actual event that caused the trapped feeling, but this isn't necessary as long as the emotion is felt and released.

I breathe deeply and consistently for about two minutes, knowing I probably have another 40 minutes to go. After a lifetime of shallow breathing, it is very difficult to do deep breathing. Your mouth gets dry, your chest hurts and your head feels dizzy. I pause for little breaks, hoping the facilitator is somewhere else in the room. Other people are doing better. The teacher is crying. The ex roadie is shouting. Aphorism woman is making strange sounds like a twittering bird. I imagine what is going on in their minds. Reliving past humiliations. Re-asserting broken boundaries. Reframing bad scenarios.

Lots of breakthroughs seem to be happening, but not to me.

I'm judging everyone in the room. I want to hit the twittering bird woman and I want to smother the ex roadie. Mostly I just want to go home, but I do feel compassion for the teacher who is weeping quietly next to me. All in all, I'm so taken up by their experience, I constantly have to remember to come back to my own – which seems to be non existent. The only feeling I have is one of complete disconnection. I can't get any sense of occupying my own body, plus I have an unpleasant dizzy feeling from the increase in oxygen. I hate feeling dizzy. I remember hideous moments in playgrounds, in dancing classes, in wine bars. The horror of feeling momentarily out of control.

Everyone else seems to be having a full on emotional meltdown now. Which of course makes me feel the exact opposite. This is not my tribe. I want to be in my ex boyfriend's tribe. The one where all the cool people hang out. The club I've been excluded from because I'm now no longer cool. What a sad thought. Cool is such an ephemeral notion. Maybe it's a good thing I no longer have to subject myself to its constantly changing template, its high bars, its...

The facilitator is on to me and comes over. He obviously thinks I am not in touch with my feelings. This isn't true. I may not be able to feel them in a workshop, where I have full permission to express them. But I can feel them perfectly well walking around the supermarket. The mere sight of the frozen peas brings a spontaneous burst of tears.

Like a dance pro, coaching a student, he asks me to breathe with him. He lifts me into a sitting position and sits opposite. I watch the rise and fall of his chest, like a metronome and follow along. I look into his eyes. It's difficult, because these eyes don't contain the usual things you expect to see. There's no sentimentality or soppiness. No pity or judgment. No arrogance or expectation. What am I looking at? Space? For a moment I have a mini mystical experience. There is nothing there... and there is everything there. This must be a bit like looking into God's eyes.

Infinite space.

Filled with love.

Deprived of anything to analyze or interpret, my mind has nowhere to go, and nothing to latch onto. It seems to burst like a bubble. I am in an altered state, beyond thought, on the other side of thought. Relief pours over me. And then, as mysteriously as it came, it is gone, and I feel a rage in my chest. Not sadness or tears or anger, but something I can only describe as full-blown fury.

I wish I could have held onto the indescribable sensation of being beyond thought, but perhaps rage is what I'm supposed to be feeling right now. This is what wants to be released. But then the rage turns quickly into sadness.

Like most Catholic girls, I find it hard to express aggression. We prefer passive aggression, because that's the pattern we've been imprinted with. We can do suffering and sadness, but when we start feeling angry we divert the energy back towards ourselves. It's a nasty masochistic imprint that I'm sure the medieval clergy were particularly pleased with. What better way to subdue thousands of people? Install a program that makes sure they subdue themselves, then you can get back to drinking the communion wine, stalking altar boys and denigrating women.

Power. The abuse of power. I think of the small girl in Africa being hacked to pieces. I think of a father searching endlessly for a child he will never see again. The anger increases. I want to kill someone.

It stops.

I'm back in the room. Part of me feels that I've failed a test. That I came face to face with an energy inside of me, but I couldn't go the distance. I'm scared of what that energy could do. Scared of losing control of the civilized veneer that is me. Perhaps this is the energy that is trying to kill me.

If so, it's only a matter of time before it wins.

TWENTY ONE

The Motherload

We break for lunch around a large refectory table. Jane is anxious to hear news of my ex boyfriend. Has he called? I say it truly is over. I tell her how I came to realize the power of my mind and its ability to project the fantasy that he still loved me. I'm wiser now... now that I know love can end with a thought. A heart beat.

Jane makes a sad face and tells me that nothing is ever over, it just changes form. We are quantum entangled with every person we have ever had a relationship with, particularly if it included sex. "That's why I've done so many letting go workshops" she laughs, implying the vast number of boyfriends she's had to cut energetic cords from.

I've only had two proper relationships, if you discount all the "You know this doesn't mean anything, it's not like we're an item" ones. Now I have to re-assess if I need to let these other guys go. I've successfully forgotten most of them. There's no way I can re-conjure them from the cosmos, so that I can consciously sever the energetic ties that bind us.

Guy – the ex roadie/personal trainer – joins the conversation. He recounts the damascene moment when he turned his life around, gave up all the one night stands and became interested in enlightenment. Jane and the astrologer nod approvingly. "Now I'm married to this incredible woman, and the sex is just amazing." This is way too much information for me.

Jane and the astrologer seem a bit jealous with the ease he has accomplished this – they are still searching for their soul mates. I am trying to do good listening, I really am, but he just comes over to me as "Basically I'm a stud." Now that it's no longer the cool thing to brag about the number of conquests, new age people have turned their competitive streak to the quality of service they deliver. Or they just rebrand casual sex by calling it Polyamory, thinking that the Greek/French overtones take away the cheapness and give it an air of sophistication.

I miss my ex boyfriend more than words can describe. None of these people feel real to me. They seem like two dimensional figures. My mind flits constantly between memory and imagination. It doesn't feel safe to occupy the space between, which is NOW. I don't want to be here. I want to stay in the memory of my relationship, because it allows me to imagine how I felt when I was with him – excited, interested, interesting. I loved that feeling. It seems like an age since I experienced it. I'm starting to doubt that I'll ever feel it again.

"How was your breathing session?" Jane asks kindly.

"A bit frustrating. It's difficult for me to get into feelings of anger without becoming really self-conscious." I move the food around on my plate.

"That's a childhood imprint. I have the same thing. We're raised to be polite and sweet". She tilts her head at Guy "whereas it's perfectly acceptable for small boys to have a full on tantrum."

He smiles back at her. "Well historically, boys grew up and went to war. It would be impossible to fight if you couldn't tap into some anger."

"But being polite and holding onto anger is so destructive to a woman's body." Jane sighs for added emphasis.

"Well, what d'you think it does to a man's body? We don't fight any more, now that drones do all the killing."

I suppose that's why Guy became a personal trainer, so he could encourage men to take their aggression out on the treadmill.

"Men do fight" abused woman says quietly. "They just find other targets."

There's a slightly awkward silence. In the world of energy, being a victim is an identity that attracts a bully. People are unsure whether to give sympathy or advice.

"Abuse" like "Love" and "Depression" is one word that covers a whole multitude of things. I've heard women at work use it to describe an incident in which a male colleague made a lewd suggestion. At the other end of the spectrum, there are women beaten within an inch of their lives.

"What was your relationship like with your mother?" Jane says to fill the silence. And because her favorite topic is the Divine Feminine. Internally I can feel myself backing away from the conversation, but I am supposed to be reclaiming my feminine energy, so rolling my eyes is not a good way to start.

Abused woman describes a co-dependent relationship with a mother who used her children as emotional support throughout a loveless marriage.

A large apple pie arrives on the table. No-one else seems as excited by this as I am, so I don't wait for them to start.

145

"I wouldn't call it co-dependency" the astrologer says. "It's more like a Faustian pact. Our mothers felt powerless, so we feel that we have to be powerless, to be like them. Otherwise we think we'll be rejected. We choose our mother's love over our own empowerment."

"You know sugar addiction is a mother issue" Jane says. She obviously remembers my eating preferences from the last workshop. "It's about self soothing. You're trying to get the love and sweetness that's missing."

"All addictions are." Guy says. "I was the same with alcohol and cocaine, back in the day."

Oh please God, not "on the road" stories. I've listened to so many of these "you had to be there" narratives that I've become a bit jaded. It was work. Hard work. The fact that it took place in a different town each day doesn't make you Jack Kerouac.

"Addiction is the cause of pain and the cure for it at the same time," Aphorism woman says.

Everyone helps themselves to pie. The astrologer looks at her plate thoughtfully. "But food *is* different from drugs and alcohol," she says. "Food makes you put on weight, so it's a defence mechanism. If we don't know how to set an energetic boundary, we build a physical one. It's an unconscious way of creating a barrier, particularly around the sex organs."

"Yes of course" Guy seems keen to bring the subject back to sex. "Second chakra. Issues around sexuality, food and creativity. They're all boundary related. Some of my clients are sex addicts who..."

"Sex addicts" snorts abused woman. "That's just an excuse."

Clearly she thinks this isn't a proper addiction. But then a lot of people think sugar isn't an addiction either. After all, how difficult is to say "I'll have the cheese board, thanks."

"I disagree" Guy says. "Addiction is a need for connection. And what better way to connect than through sex."

"I have such a difficult relationship with my mother" the teacher says, clearly attempting to interrupt Guy and head off an impending argument. "I'm 45 and I'm *still* trying to honour my own choices, where she's concerned. I'm fine with everyone else, but she makes me feel guilty, so I constantly betray myself rather than upset her."

"Exactly" Jane says. "Our mothers didn't know how to establish boundaries, so they went into monumental levels of sacrifice, over extending themselves, then feeling resentful about it. Of course they can't speak about the resentment because they've not been taught self expression, so they end up guilt tripping everyone instead.

"But they weren't free to make their own choices in the first place." The teacher sounded exasperated "So I do have compassion for her, but that doesn't stop me feeling angry with her at the same time."

"A mother is a person who seeing there are only four pieces of pie for five people, promptly announces she never did care for pie," Aphorism woman says to no-one in particular.

I don't know where I am with this conversation. On the one hand, mothers seem to get a really bad rap these days and on the other, they are seen as the future of the planet. In their deified form of course – the Divine Mother. The Goddess. The woman who's been healed of her wounds and is no longer a victim.

The world needs this woman to show up as a matter of some urgency.

I don't remember much about my mother. She died when I was sixteen, and because I seem to have sleep walked through most of my childhood, I can't even remember what the relationship was like. I was a rebel, so I suspect I rejected the notion of being mothered. There's obviously a problem here. A contradictory push-pull of "want... but don't want." A disturbance in the force, as Obi-wan Kenobi would say.

I suddenly remember being on the cold train station, and the feeling I had, just before my life collapsed. *I wanted someone to mother me, to tell me everything was going to be alright.* They say that soldiers dying on the battlefield only call out for two things – God or their mother. Perhaps God is a Goddess after all, the cosmic equivalent of an earthly mother. Never judging, always ready to love, soothe and kiss it better. Unconditional compassion.

I want help, but I don't know how to ask for it, and if the help comes in the form of energy, I certainly don't know how to receive it. I feel exhausted, exasperated, defeated...

I realize the others are looking at me. "What?"

"Oh I thought you were about to say something" Astrology woman smiles. Perhaps she had noticed my growing distress, my intense stare and my need to say...

"Does anyone want that last piece of pie?"

TWENTY TWO

Story Time

After a break to allow the food to digest, we file back in for the afternoon session. I don't know how I feel about "workshop conversations." It's clear that people are becoming more conscious about the need to transcend their psychology, open their heart and heal their relationship to the feminine... and this is a very good thing. These types of conversation would never have happened a few generations ago, when we shook hands and nobody spoke about their feelings. However, they sometimes feel artificial and full of jargon.

I suppose in our fast moving world, jargon is a useful short cut. Words don't adequately sum up ANYTHING in the energy realm, and we have to put names on things to provide a shared context. But it also means that if you pick up some fancy new jargon, you can leap frog over the necessary work involved in actually changing the dysfunctional patterns.

When I hear people discussing "their abundance issue" now, I either tune out completely or I want to scream "Just say what you mean – you're broke." Having an "abundance issue" of course means it's not your fault and maybe there's a part of me that actually likes finding fault.

Jargon allows you into a club. When I was younger, I was guilty of rock and roll jargon. I figured if I knew the right words, people wouldn't realize I didn't have a clue what I was talking about, and they'd let me stay in the club.

Now I seem to have joined the spiritual high club.

I'm lying on the floor in a room that resembles a nursery full of children waiting for bedtime stories, like the bunch of lost boys who have idealized their perfect mother in Wendy. I imagine what's going through the teacher's head. Scenes from her classroom featuring unruly children? Compassion and anger competing for supremacy, just as it did with her mother.

Looking over at aphorism woman, I get images of a 1950s mother holding a tray of baked goods like Betty Crocker, smiling in an exaggerated sort of way. "Nice" is just so irritating.

I move onto the ex roadie. He's quiet for a change. I wonder what emotion he's struggling with. Jealousy that he never got to be on stage himself? Or self doubt? Perhaps he was like the *Tiswas* character, desperate to prove something.

I was there! I mattered. I was necessary.

This makes me feel sad. An old memory flashes through my mind of a heavy metal gig. Insufficient power supply at the venue, required the last minute hiring of a generator, which arrived in the nick of time – but without any fuel. Everyone was panicking because without the extra power there would be no lighting rig, a major tantrum of rock star proportions, and a cancelled show. One roadie volunteered to syphon diesel from the truck. This meant putting a tube into the fuel tank and sucking the air out until the diesel appeared in the tube, then quickly inserting the tube into the generator, allowing the fuel to transfer.

Everyone stood around anxiously hoping this would work. He bent over the tube and started to breath in. The diesel came out too quickly and he swallowed a large mouthful. The others rushed to grab the tube and put it in the generator. There were cheers all round as the fuel gauge rose. Meanwhile the lone roadie was vomiting against the wheel arch of the truck. He looked ashen. He had proved himself, but his heroic act was short lived in the rush to get on to the next thing.

I was there. I mattered. I was brave.

Breathe. Keep breathing. The music is loud and primal. Bass drums and didgeridoos. I love this music.

Jane starts shouting and banging her hands and feet on the floor, like a two year old having a tantrum. The facilitator turns the music up louder, as the energy in the room builds. I can't imagine how to get sound to come out of my mouth without it sounding ridiculous. I am too self conscious.

After lunch Jane had urged me to do some work on self-love, to help with the sugar addiction. She builds self-love into her daily routine by looking in the mirror every morning and telling her reflection how much she loves her. This just conjures up images of Snow White's mad stepmother. "Mirror, mirror on the wall, you are the fairest of them all." The self doesn't need any more love... because it's insatiable.

The soul needs love. The kind of love that's freely available in the energy world. But we need to become good conductors of energy before we can access it.

In the real world a conductor is someone (usually male) who controls and directs an orchestra with his little baton. (Now there's a metaphor to conjure with). In the energy world a good conductor is something that allows energy to move through it.

People in general are bad conductors of the energy of Love. They create rubber like barriers in the mind and heart.

The mind fears losing control to something it can't see, so spends a lot of time trying to control things it CAN see – money, food, social media. Compulsive behaviour acts as an earthing rod for the energy. This stops the flow.

The heart fears the emotions of failure, shame and rejection so instead of becoming soul conscious, it spends a lot of time being self conscious. This definitely stops the flow.

Stops the love.

Some people, like Jane, advise depressed people to love themselves, exactly as they are. I suppose this is a bit "fake it till you make it". But you can't fake things in the energy world.

Others suggest that the best thing to do is achieve a target – lose weight, get a makeover, strive for success, because these things bring self-esteem. But if being slim, beautiful and successful was the answer, Marilyn Monroe would have kept the lid on the pill bottle, Robin Williams would have left the dressing gown cord in the closet and Sylvia Plath would have put the chicken in the oven, instead of her own head...

Breathe. You've stopped breathing. Again.

We need soul esteem, not self esteem. But how do we even meet the soul? Karl Jung believed the energy world revealed itself in dreams. In life we cling to one identity (good person!) and repress its opposite (bad person!). If we are rebellious or going through a gothic phase, we can choose the opposite (The lure of dark glamour!) Our dreams reveal aspects of ourselves that we have hidden.

If we dream of a happy puppy, an axe murderer, a frightened child, and a vain stepmother, then according to Jung, we are not one, but ALL of these things. We are all the characters in the story. It's no wonder we resist becoming more conscious.

I don't want to talk to myself in the mirror, as this would surely indicate a decline into madness and narcissism. Perhaps underneath my tough exterior, I am Snow White, the innocent child. After all, I actually do like to stay home all day, and I love little people (except when they appear in coffee shops). I'm not great with a dustpan and brush but two out of three isn't bad. Who else is in the story? The huntsman. A shiver runs down my spine. The huntsman takes Snow White into the forest to cut out her heart. I am the huntsman.

"You're not breathing." The facilitator is by my side again.

"I find it really difficult."

Why am I the only person in the room who is struggling with something so basic?

"Your mind doesn't like to do something unfamiliar and it creates resistance." He bangs a metal tuning fork and places it on my heart. Sound waves go through my body, pulling my attention downwards. It feels good to get out of my head. That hippie euphemism for drug taking. "I need to get out of my head, man."

"Come back" the facilitator again. It's uncanny, he can literally see my thoughts, or maybe he just watches the energy move from my heart, back to my head again. "Stay here. Stay here with me and breathe." I open my eyes and look into his. The same compassion. The same neutrality of expression. How does he not get exasperated by such a hopeless student?

He beats the tuning fork again and places it on my heart. Something inside me lets go. I surrender my will into his. Sadness pours out of me. It's more than sadness, it's sadness mixed with exasperation and exhaustion. I am tired of fighting for my life. I want to curl up in a quiet corner somewhere and go to sleep for a hundred years.

A couple of hours later, while everyone is saying their goodbyes, the facilitator takes me to one side. "I can see the problem you're having," he said. "I struggled with depression myself, years ago."

I immediately burst into tears. Two sentences reduce me to a sobbing wreck. It's not the sentences of course, it's the feeling that somebody actually understands. I didn't even speak about the depression and yet he knows exactly what I'm going through. This isn't a simple acknowledgement. It's a feeling of being connected at a deep level. It's not "I see you… down there, well the dim outline of you anyway." Instead, it's "I see you, right here, in front of me."

"How did you get out of it?" I say.

"You could try an Ayahuasca ceremony."

The thought I had in the park comes back. Maybe it was a premonition after all. Some other form of intelligence was calling me to it. The intelligence contained in the dark underworld of the ground. In the roots of the plants of the Amazon. The idea was attractive and abhorrent in equal measure. I'm too scared. I hate feeling dizzy. I won't be in control. And yet, the dark is where I currently live.

"What makes you say that?"

"You need some way of by passing your mind. Emotions are held in the body, but you don't have much of a connection to your body. Your energy is very cut off at the neck."

"Well yeah, I do live in my head most of the time, so I don't get too many messages from my body… Or my soul" I add as an afterthought. "I feel like I'm just witnessing my life, as if it's a movie, and I'm not actually in it." I take a deep breath. "And I have absolutely no energy."

"Well, I do believe depression is a spiritual crisis, not a mental one. The reason I got into breath work is because you can't fix the mind with the mind."

"Exactly!"

"Obviously you can tame the mind. Meditation is great for that."

I make an exasperated face.

"You're trying to run before you can walk. If you have a loud mind and a quiet soul, you have to start slowly. Otherwise it's like expecting an unruly teenager, to listen. Particularly one who had no training as a child."

This makes sense, but it feels like an impossible trap. My soul wants to be in gym club but it needs to get fit before it can join.

"Maybe one day I'll be able to do it."

"But not this day." He smiles back. "That's why breath work is good, because it brings the body on board. There's a lot of intelligence in your body, join that to your soul and you've got a winning combination. A bit like a pincer attack, forcing the mind to submit.

"But I can't even do the breathing properly. There's too much resistance." I'm feeling defeated again.

"Your mind has probably over ruled the body on so many occasions that you've severed the connection. I bet you've always been able to cope with chaos."

I nod my head.

"Stress."

More nodding.

"Working when you're ill and should probably be in hospital."

"Badge of honour." I smile.

"Bet you thought you could get away with it indefinitely."

I can feel the tears in my chest and try to swallow them down.

"We think we can control life with our mind," he says softly. The eyes again. Don't look in his eyes or you'll be completely unhinged. "But you weren't listening to your soul."

One tear spills over and makes its way down my cheek.

"Bet you're listening now."

TWENTY THREE

The Waiting Game

I'm in the park. I called the recommended shaman and we spoke for some time. He asked me loads of questions before clearing me to take part in the next ceremony. This is reassuring. Often when I book onto a seminar, the only question I'm asked is "What's the long number on the front of the card?"

We went through my history, and talked about the depression. Luckily I am not taking any medication, as this would immediately rule me out from attending. My timing is good (serendipity) because the ceremony takes place in ten days, so there is just enough time to do the necessary preparation.

There's preparation.

Ayahuasca is medicine for the soul, not the body. In fact it's called "the vine of souls". Whereas medicine for the body tends to be masculine – chemicals, technology and surgical procedures – medicine for the soul is more feminine. The masculine approach is all about focus. Find the enemy (like a tumor) and attack it. But we are holistic systems. The tumor is connected to the rest of the body, which is connected to the etheric body, where the pattern lies, waiting to repeat itself.

Masculine strategy is great at winning battles and losing wars.

Ayahuasca is a holistic solution, because it contains an intelligence that understands the complexities of connectivity – beyond the narrow focus of the mind.

We love the mind because it's just so darned clever, but it's also extremely limited, and we forget that. If you like playing chess, you'll be really impressed with a genius chess-playing robot. "OMG how fast can it make calculations! It's SO awesome! And it makes me a better chess player!" We get so carried away that we forget that playing chess is a small part of life (or it should be if you actually have a life). We forget that the chess-playing robot is actually quite rubbish at playing football, or cooking an omelet. We become blind to its limitations.

Meanwhile the soul is trying to get us into a more expanded world of different experiences. A world of joy, not cleverness. A world of love, not interesting data. I want to be part of that world. I don't want to live in the prison my mind has created. So I will overcome my fear of losing control. I will take part in this ancient ceremony that shaman have been conducting for thousands of years.

There is, however, a long list of requirements that I must adhere to before taking part, most important of which is an extreme diet. Not extreme as in fasting – I can eat as much as I like of the foods on the list. Just extreme as in there are no foods on the list I would actually want to eat.

Most important and seemingly impossible of all the food restrictions is NO SUGAR. No sugar of any kind. Also no salt, alcohol, coffee, caffeine, spices, onion, garlic, dairy, meat, citrus fruits. In other words bland, bland and more bland. Plant medicine is very subtle and the sensory overload on the body has to be turned down, right down in order for it to work properly.

Also no sex. (This part is easy given my current single status) and no masturbation (also easy, don't have the energy). No television (great I don't have to be reminded of how unfriendly the world is on the evening news). Above all, no chemical medicine. No anti-depressants, sleep inducers, or mood enhancers of any kind.

I am already feeling desperate for a coffee and cake fix, and it's only mid morning of the first day. I have no idea how I am going to get through the next week. Looking around at the trees, shrubs and flowers in the park, they seem harmless enough. But maybe this is my first introduction to paradox. The plant world is both innocent and wise; gentle and tough; flexible and consistent.

In other words, it can contain opposing forces. If I want to be a better container for energy, the plant kingdom may be a wiser teacher than any academic institution. I can't learn about the feminine in words, because it's beyond words. I have to experience it.

Perhaps a trip to an art gallery will help take my mind off things. My drawing meditation has become half hearted, so I could certainly benefit from some artistic inspiration. If I download a bus timetable, I won't have to go near the underground.

Much later (London buses iconic but slow) I'm in the Tate Britain standing in front of The Lady of Shallot. The Victorians were certainly genius at portraying the damsel archetype. Pre Raphaelites loved nothing more than to paint red haired beauties gazing wistfully out of windows. We forget how boring these women's lives must have been. Reading, needlepoint and being beautiful. Watching the world, watching men running it, watching children grow up. No wonder women of my generation couldn't wait to join the men's club.

My fear of being boring propelled me away from this version of the feminine, but part of my soul craves the romance.

Elaine (The Lady of Shallot) went one stage further and watched the world through a mirror, not a window. She was under a spell that would cause her death if she interacted with the real world. I am living the opposite version of this story – living in the real world, but cut off from the energy one. My mind seems to believe that if I interact directly with the divine, I will die.

Of course I won't actually die, but the power of my mind will be somewhat diminished so that my heart and soul can have a bigger say in what's going on. I suppose to the mind, being cut down to size, would feel a bit like dying.

This is a very bad spell to be under.

Elaine became accustomed to her routine life of weaving and waiting but was doomed when Lancelot appeared in the mirror. Being a romantic, she couldn't stop herself from wanting more direct contact. This invoked the spell and she died while floating down the river looking really beautiful and very tragic.

I'm romantic. Romance isn't love, it's the anticipation of love, which is a different kind of waiting. Not bored waiting, but butterflies in the stomach waiting. Damsels become addicted to this feeling, but it's not confined to romantics – gamblers become addicted to the same feeling. They don't care about the winning, or the money. Gamblers are addicted to the feeling they get, just before the ball lands on the roulette wheel.

We are drawn to the feeling of "almost but not yet", drawn to what is about to manifest. It's an exciting space where anything could happen. A highly charged energy with infinite possibilities.

We could live in this feeling more often if we were connected to the divine. This is what the energy world is all about. But we choose to limit its expression by projecting it onto a boyfriend, a roulette wheel or more general risk taking. Then we can convince ourselves that at least we have some control over the process.

I look at Elaine in her boat and feel a strong connection to my inner damsel. I wished she could have found a way to break the spell, but I'm pleased that she's no longer waiting, trapped in a tower like a caged bird.

I am half sick of shadows, said the Lady of Shallot.

If the journey of the damsel is to swop romantic love for divine love, then the journey of the rebel must be to swop counterfeit freedom for real freedom. This is my intention for the Ayahuasca. I want it to set me free. That's one giant leap for a human being, but perhaps one small step for a really smart plant.

I'm on day four of the diet. It's really hard. The only way I can manage, is to sleep as much as possible. This is not too difficult because now that I'm deprived of vanilla lattes in the morning, I can't get out of bed anyway. I wake up, remember my predicament and groan. My low energy levels have plummeted even further without the caffeine. I'm also crying constantly.

On the one hand, this is a reasonable response. After all, I am doing something difficult. But on the other hand, I feel pathetic with my first world problem. There are millions of people who've had no more than a bowl of rice a day for years.

I count how many times I reach for something to numb my experience of the world. Sugar. Coffee. Alcohol. Social Media. I constantly need to distract myself. I'm also becoming aware of a gnawing sensation in the pit of my stomach, which feels like hunger but isn't. It twists and turns and won't allow me to settle. I can't write, because I can't concentrate. It's even difficult to read. I find myself going over the same paragraph again and again as the words dance in front of my eyes, but don't register in my brain.

I'm feeling anxious. This ceremony feels like my last ditch attempt at claiming my life back. I'm worried that my expectations are too high. Things tend not to work if you have expectations – lottery tickets, love. Oh God, love. Don't think about him. Too late. I want to turn back the clock, do everything differently. I would have no expectations. I could live in the moment. Never ask why. Never ask when. Never, ever look for clues.

I could just see if he's posted anything on social media. Stop! He's yet another addiction. Step away from the computer! Is it time to go to bed yet? It's 8.00pm and if I have a really long bath then that will be 9.00pm, which is almost a normal time to go to bed. Not normal if you get up at midday obviously but I can conveniently forget, that as I clutch at any straw I can find.

TWENTY FOUR

Let's Do This

I'm here. I made it through the week and I'm finally here. Nervous and a bit scared, I meet the others and we swop stories of who found what the most difficult thing to give up. It's a different crew to the usual workshop attendees. Notably there are twice as many men as women. This makes me feel more comfortable.

It's not that I have a problem with the feminine. I just don't know what it is yet. I keep being presented with versions that I can't relate to, and these personalities of the feminine just make me more and more rebellious.

Women have long dominated the arena of self-development. Some people put this down to the fact that life is generally working out OK for men, so they don't feel the need to develop themselves. When questioned, they may admit to having a few problems under the hood, but there's still "power in the engine" so "if it ain't completely broke, don't fix it." Men appreciate car analogies and would probably go to a self-development workshop if it was facilitated by Jeremy Clarkson.

Others suggest that the lack of men in the new-age fields is down to fear. They like to hang out in places where they can excel – battle fields, board rooms, football pitches. They've been programmed to win and women tend to win at new-age stuff, because they're much better at the jargon.

If the car breaks down, we don't feel comfortable when a woman starts talking about the idling speed of the carburetor, and we feel even less comfortable if a man rolls his eyes and blames mercury retrograde.

Words are a big problem.

Personalities are another problem. When you put the two together, it's really hard to break a paradigm.

Anyway it's interesting to see lots of male faces in a ceremony dedicated to inner healing and connection to the divine. There are several people who work in the media, some from I.T, and a few Burners (people who have attended Burning Man festival). Burning Man is currently giving the new-age community a contemporary upgrade, which is a good thing, because let's face it, the new-age is now middle aged. It's become sedate and ineffective.

A lot of new-age people wear the clothes (does my aura look big in this?) but don't do much follow through (I can't start a revolution, I have a meeting with my therapist and the moon is in my seventh house).

I love the Burners. They're making alternative culture edgy again, like it was in the sixties, when we all agreed that opening the doors of perception was a good thing. This of course, was back before Jim Morrison died, Pink Floyd broke up and they made a president out of a movie actor. Back then, there was a lot of energy about. It's referred to as "the SPIRIT of the 60s" for a reason.

What happened to the energy of the love revolution? The power elite became threatened, and with good reason. They owned corporations. When the consumers they were selling to started singing *All You Need is Love*, they didn't see this as a good omen for future profits. Luckily they also owned the media, and a bunch of advertising and P.R. companies. They came up with a different idea – FEAR. They marketed the crap out of it and pretty soon Brand Fear became the market leader. The spirit of the sixties got relegated to the back shelf, along with Velvet Underground, beat poetry and tie-dye.

Occasionally in the past few decades, optimism has reared its head again. But it's been squashed with another strategy that has proven to be equally effective – ridicule. Currently Russell Brand is taking on the power elite. His arguments are clear and obvious – he asks why they are selling guns to terrorists, and giving bonuses to corrupt bankers. The sum total of their counter arguments amounts to personal attack. If this exchange took place in a children's playground, it would sound a bit like the following:

Russell: I'm curious as to why you just stole the chocolate biscuit from my lunch box and sold it the kid whose mum forgot to pack him a sandwich... for six times the original price. Would you like to offer an explanation?

Media: Hahahahaha... you're such a dickhead, your lunch box is a joke, and you look like a girl.

When Larry Harvey set up the Burning Man festival, he did so with no rules, just principles. Like radical inclusion (welcome and respect strangers), Sharing (giving with no expectation of return), Co-operation and collaboration (absolutely no sponsorship or advertising), Radical self expression (No dress code), Leave no trace (clear up your shit – ALL of it, so it looks like you weren't even there in the first place).

The establishment said... Hahahahahahaha... that will NEVER work! People are lazy, suspicious, greedy, out for number one and UNBELIEVABLY messy – particularly in large groups.

So what actually happens? Each year more people attend, the principles are adhered to, the creativity is astonishing, an entire city is built and dismantled, and after the event there isn't any litter. It's time for a new idea about how to build communities that are not based on competition, greed and self-interest.

Looking around the kitchen at my fellow participants, they don't look like wounded souls. They're successful, curious individuals who are searching for a better way to do life. They know the old ways don't work. They've seen through the bullshit pipe dream that corporations and the media have been selling.

"Ah," I hear the skeptics say "but Ayahuasca is just a hallucinogenic drug, so isn't this a case of, *same shit different day?*"

The terms *drugs* and *medicine* are interchangeable. Medical professionals tend to use drugs created by humans, in laboratories (so some of these are aptly named *Frankenstein drugs)*. Shamans use medicine created by nature, in forests.

Drugs/medicine of both kinds can treat the body or the mind, but not the soul. Only plant medicine can help in this area, because only plant medicine is still connected to the whole of consciousness. Humans severed that connection when we evolved our neo-cortex – our thinking mind. Ayahuasca has been used for thousands of years for both healing and divination.

Divination is a funny word. The dictionary describes it "to foresee, or be inspired by God." Now that we know God is not a person but a vastly superior form of intelligence, we could really do with some divination. Not just because our intelligence has made a mess of the planet, but because finding our purpose in life will make us happy. We aren't buying the "one size fits all purpose" sold by corporations – money, house, career, spouse. We want the purpose our soul craves – the ability to express our unique essence in a way that serves others and delights ourselves.

Recently Ayahuasca has been given a bad rap because young people are arriving in droves in South America – some conscious (who want spiritual awareness or spiritual expansion) some unconscious (who want to get off their face because they've heard it's the ultimate trip). A few people have died. So it's important to add some context.

Peru is a very poor country. Wherever there is poverty, there will be opportunism. If you've spent a lifetime trying to earn a few dollars selling peaches by the roadside but people drive past, in order to spend thousands of dollars on vine leaves a bit further down the road, you're going to swop the sign over your store, pretty damn quickly. It takes years of time and incredible discipline to become a shaman, but when the rewards are this high, it encourages charlatans.

We live in a capitalist society. Jewelry shops are sometimes ransacked by thieves. But we don't blame the diamonds for the damage.

It's impossible to overdose on Ayahuasca or be harmed by it in any way, when the ceremony is conducted with consciousness, by experienced shamans.

It's time to meet them.

TWENTY FIVE

She

So here we are, obedient students of the plant. We've fulfilled all the conditions for entry into the classroom. Our bodies have been cleansed of human interference. There are no chemical drugs (medicinal or recreational) in our system, and no residues of synthetic or manufactured foods.

We are hungry, but we have to fast now until the end of the ceremony, which will be around 3am. It's time to individually meet with the husband and wife team who will be facilitating the ceremony. I'll call them Richard and Karen to show that in real life shamans often have normal names, rather than Flying Eagle or Golden Aphrodite. (Also in honour of the Carpenters because they let Tony Peluso play one of the best guitar solos of all time at the end of *Goodbye to Love*).

It's important to have discernment when choosing a shaman. Always follow a combination of personal recommendation and intuition.

The ceremony room is dark and womb like. All windows and sky-lights have been blacked out. Sleeping bags and mats line either side. Richard and Karen's mats are at the top of the room, and are surrounded with a huge range of musical instruments, tuning forks, incense, oils, pipes, pouches of herbs and tobacco and two large jars of dark liquid. I had already spoken to them on the phone, but seeing how they were together I realized that I had finally found something I'd been searching for...

An example of true partnership.

Too late to prove a point to my ex boyfriend of course. Look! It does exist! Like all valuable, intangible things, their relationship is hard to explain in words. It's one of deep love, mutual respect and profound connection – without an ounce of sentimentality. I am about to go through some kind of transcendent experience and these people are my guides? This is like winning the workshop lottery. My mind says "what about that fear of nausea and dizziness" but I silence that voice and take my place on the mat ready for the ceremony to begin.

One by one we go to the front of the room, sit in front of Karen to be anointed with oil, then sit in front of Richard to receive a cup full of the dark liquid. Once we are all back in our places, various incantations and prayers are said and we all drink together. The low lighting is now turned off and we are in complete darkness. Richard starts to sing the Icaros – songs taught to the shamans by the spirits of the plants. They are used to call in the higher energies. They are also used to remove dark energies and to seal the room in a cocoon of protection.

An hour later most people in the room are having an experience. Some people are vomiting, some are crying, some are blissful. I feel nothing, apart from a cold loneliness. This is not what I anticipated. It's the expectation thing of course. If you build yourself up, disappointment is inevitable. What is wrong with me?

Karen comes over and offers me more medicine. I gulp it quickly because it's the most disgusting thing I have ever drunk. It has the consistency of thick cough syrup and a foul acrid taste which sticks to the inside of your mouth. I curl up in a ball feeling nauseous. As I lie there, for what seems like an age, Richard and Karen play a variety of musical instruments and sing in two part harmony. Their voices are exquisite, a perfect blend of high, low and what can only be described as "other worldly" sounds. The songs are the only comforting part of the experience. I want it to end. I desperately want it to end.

Ayahuasca is not a hallucinogenic in the traditional meaning of the word. It induces consciousness, giving you more access to your true self. It doesn't alter your external reality. You can get up and walk to the toilet without seeing pink elephants or the ground moving under your feet. It strips away illusions, allowing a glimpse into an inner reality, underneath the egoic structures that the mind has created.

My mind has obviously constructed its version of reality on very solid foundations – thick concrete, possibly containing a few dead bodies. I've always been an attention to detail person. If I have to construct an ego in order to survive, I'm not going to make a half arsed job of it.

Eventually I hear Richard say that it's the end of the ceremony. Some people go to the kitchen to eat bland soup, others stay on their mats blissfully transitioning from medicine induced dreaming to normal dreaming. I get up and go for a walk outside. There are thousands of stars, but I'm in no state to appreciate them. I'm angry and frustrated, and decide the whole idea of being here is a complete mistake.

The following day all the participants sit in a circle and share their experiences – journeys where they met deceased relatives, angels or spirit guides, and saw visions of incredible colours. Some describe a sense of really knowing who they are and their place in the universe. I feel disillusioned, cranky and tired. But I don't share this. I decide to leave in the afternoon and skip the next ceremony.

We break for lunch – omelet (no seasoning) and salad (no dressing). I decide to tell Richard and Karen I am leaving, rather than sneaking off and sending an email later with some made up excuse. This is progress, and evidence that I have at least added one new skill to my emotional repertoire.

Richard and Karen don't force me to stay. They want what's best for me. I don't feel judged, I just feel their love. After a chat over a cup of tea, I decide to stay after all. I have no idea why, other than fear of the despair that awaits me when I return home.

Hippocrates once said "If someone wishes for good health, one must first ask oneself if he is ready to do away with the reasons for his illness. Only then is it possible to help him." You can tell when things are the truth, because they are unchanged by fashion, culture and time. Hippocrates was born in 460 BC, so there's a good chance there's truth in his words. I know at least one of my reasons is the need to run away from things, so perhaps running towards them will help.

I now have a free afternoon to meditate on some questions. By having such a lonely, detached experience, what is the Ayahuasca trying to communicate to me?

At 7.00pm we file into the room as before, receive a cup of medicine and go back to our mats. Doubt creeps in. Maybe I stayed for the second night because I'm a people pleaser. I like Richard and Karen, and don't want them to think badly of me. On the other hand, maybe they don't realize how bad my predicament is. I need a jack hammer not a plant to break the stranglehold of my mind. This is going to be another long night.

One hour into the ceremony I'm experiencing nothing but loneliness. I take another cup and feel extreme nausea. I feel as if I've just stepped off a roundabout. My head is spinning and my stomach churning. I hate this. It's a waking nightmare. Richard says I'm ready for a third cup. I can't do it. I feel like a sea-sick sailor who's being asked to swallow a prairie oyster. It's impossible. "Drink it and you'll purge what's trying to come up, then you can drink some more." The thought of relief from the nausea allows me to drink the third drink and I immediately vomit. I feel marginally better. But now he wants me to drink more. Somehow I get it down and crawl back to my mat, hoping to sleep it off.

I don't sleep. Now that I've purged, I can sense the medicine is free to make its way into my body. It feels like a snake, stealthy, slow moving, searching out corners, looking, looking. This is so weird. There is a presence in my body. An intelligence that is not me. Now it's communicating with me. It seems to be saying something like "Just hang on, I've got this." The nausea has returned, only now it's not in my stomach or my throat, it's down, deep in my intestines, in my pelvis. I can't be sick because I've already vomited whatever was in my system and I haven't eaten for ten hours. But then the heaving begins.

I am now on my hands and knees kneeling over a bucket. Nothing comes out of me, but that doesn't stop the heaving. It's not my stomach that's contracting, it's as if the snake has coiled itself around the double helix of my DNA and is squeezing it mercilessly. I asked to be reverse engineered, but this torture wasn't quite what I had in mind. In between the intense retching, the spirit of the plant seems to be coaching me, willing me to stay with it. I have no choice, no control whatsoever. Richard is now on one side of me, and Karen on the other. They are singing, beating drums, shaking rattles, humming, whistling. Karen is making strange ethereal sounds. Richard is answering with low guttural ones.

I am in labor having contractions without any recourse to pain relief and without the imminent joy of a new baby. That's how I feel, surrounded by two midwives, trying to vomit up a demon that has its roots anchored in my hips. Now the contractions of the dry heaving are stronger. It's difficult to breath. I feel like I'm dying because something is attempting to turn me completely inside out. I can hear myself making strange animal noises in between the tears and then it happens... one long, giant internal twist, as if some super human force is squeezing the final drops of water from a damp rag, and I vomit a mass of black liquid.

Karen strokes my back, says "Good job", covers me with a blanket and leaves me curled up on the mat. I feel like I'm falling, not into a rabbit hole, but into a state of complete bliss. I feel free, happy and euphoric. I am in awe, in the truest sense of the word. This intelligence in my body is somehow communicating with me. It's wise, majestic, playful, kind, strong, loving, welcoming...

And it's undeniably feminine.

TWENTY SIX

The Physics of Love

When I wake up, and open my eyes, there are a couple of things I notice in quick succession. The black cloud is no longer there and the heaviness is gone. I feel light as a feather. I don't have to drag myself from the bed with super human effort, just a slight breeze from the open window would be sufficient to lift me to a vertical position. I don't want to move in case I break the magic of this extraordinary morning. I'd forgotten what it was like to wake up, not wanting to die, so I want to stay here as long as possible, reviewing the previous night.

After my seemingly endless labour and purging, I rested in a euphoric haze, bathed in a feeling of love. It's difficult to describe this type of love, because as humans, our understanding of love is limited to the way we feel when we love something or someone. There's a sweetness of emotion, when we think about them.

We rarely describe it the other way around. In fact, when someone loves us, it can feel burdensome. And the idea of something abstract loving us, is absurd.

We may say that we want to be loved, but we actually lack the ability. Receiving feels awkward – whether that's receiving praise, receiving gifts or receiving love. They're like hot potatoes that need to be immediately thrown back. If we get a compliment we brush it away or fire one straight back at the other person. Gifts make us reach for the ledger in our mind that tells us where we are on the credits and debits balance sheet. If the gift is expensive we feel we owe the other person. If it's cheap, we feel resentful.

So it's natural for us to extend this behaviour to love. Our love is a transaction. Give and take. Sometimes we're the subject, sometimes the object. And our mind is the sentry keeping the score.

Yet somewhere in our psyche, we long for a different kind of love. One that contains subject, object and the space between. The Lover, the Loved and the Love. An unconditional, fierce love that ravishes every cell in our body. A tsunami, that has the power to sweep away our mind, with its endless capacity to watch what is going on. We don't want to watch any more, we want to participate.

This love is an experience of union. And that's what the Ayahuasca felt like.

I have no idea why we have such resistance to this kind of love. Perhaps we don't feel worthy of it – we think we're flawed, fake or not good enough. We've been indoctrinated for thousands of years with bad prayers "Oh Lord I am not worthy of your love but just say the word and I'll be healed".

Perhaps we're scared of being overwhelmed by something so good that we'd be frightened of losing it. After all, we hate losing. We don't really buy into the adage "Better to have loved and lost than never to have loved at all," we just buy the fridge magnet or write the words on a Facebook status.

What I realized during my Ayahuasca ceremony was how much resistance I had to BEING loved. It was easy for my mind to keep up border patrol. People were dispatched, in case they became needy. Praise was thrown off seconds after it was received. (*It's nothing. Really*). Philosophies were rejected (*Love myself? Oh please*).. That's why I became so captivated by counterfeit love – romance, power struggles and the yearning of unrequited love.

Like many independent people, I have tough defenses. It was ironic therefore, that what broke through my rigid mind was seemingly the most powerless thing on the planet – a plant.

The love, when it came in was strange, wonderful and not like any love I'd experienced. We're back with the problem of words. It isn't accurate to say "like love, but bigger". Size is meaningless, once we go beyond our three dimensional experience of reality. On the other side of the divide, paradox rules. The Kingdom of Heaven can be found in a mustard seed. No wonder there was some confusion in transcribing the teachings of Jesus. It seems he was trying to describe quantum physics to fishermen.

So back to the feeling of the love. Because I can't describe it, I'd have to say it was love at a higher frequency. And because of the higher frequency, it encompassed paradox. I became the lover, the loved and the love. It was profound, but at the same time very playful. Many mystics have said that when they finally saw God she was laughing.

In addition to the love, there was the beauty. Exquisite, geometric patterns were superimposed on everything I looked at. It all felt alive, vital and connected. The room seemed to be a superconductor of energy, as if electrons, released from their orbit around a nucleus were free to move in a joyous dance, before returning home.

The music echoed this. Richard's deep voice provided the core strength, allowing Karen's voice to fly free, play, and improvise secure in the knowledge that she could always find her way back to him. It was the perfect union of masculine and feminine, each holding a space for the other. Containing and setting free. Containing and setting free. Breathing in and breathing out.

The spirit of the plant communicated non-verbally, but somehow I was able to understand it. Now that the resistance was gone, unconditional love and life force moved through my body inviting me into this great cosmic dance.

I was aware of the fact that I had been smiling for a long time, and yet my face didn't feel tired. The smile didn't seem to be coming from my cheek muscles but from some deeper impulse. I had no agenda to understand anything. I was happy just being, just hanging out in this container of bliss, peace and joy. I had finally let go and fallen into the void.

You can't go after the feminine, you can only create the necessary environment. And after that, it comes for you.

As I got out of bed, I remembered my experience of feeling isolated and angry, the night before. Now I knew what the Ayahuasca had been communicating. It was reflecting back to me the original thought that had created the pattern, long before my conscious memory. "This is a mistake. I came to the wrong planet. I don't like it here. I've changed my mind. I want to go home!" If you swop planet for workshop, this pretty much sums up my experience of the day before. Pattern repeat... same shit different day. I dropped a stitch before I was even born. No wonder I often felt so disconnected. I'm not "all in". I never have been "all in."

We come from a higher frequency dimension, to experience life in a lower frequency one. Perhaps this is a grand adventure, a bit of fun, or a noble mission to do something meaningful, and assist the evolution process. However, once we get here we forget who we are. Except (like Neo in the Matrix), there's a little splinter in our mind, niggling, telling us that things aren't quite right.

This splinter causes a sadness, a yearning for something we can't put into words. Either we fall into that sadness or we repress it in order to become fully functioning humans. Life becomes auto-matic, devoid of deep feelings, something we sleep walk through. But as the effect of the imbalance in masculine and feminine energy reaches its zenith, we are all being nudged to wake up.

TWENTY SEVEN

No Time like the Present

I'd like to say that I left the retreat centre, came home and lived happily ever after, but I'm writing about real life, not life according to Walt Disney.

Walt Disney, along with all the other great story tellers, based his films on The Hero's Journey. This is an archetypal story arc in which the protagonist leaves one place, goes on a journey to reach another place, and is transformed along the way. Cinderella is a classic example. Rags to riches. Unloved to loved. Shabby to beautiful.

Walt never did sequels, in which the Prince is less liberal with the romantic gestures and spends all his time on an iPhone, while Cinders has lost her 20" waist and has a couple of kids who are difficult to control.

The story of transformation is compelling. Robert McKee, the Hollywood King of Story, goes so far as to say if there hasn't been a change of value (fear to courage, hope to despair, hate to love) between the beginning and end of a story, then you haven't got a film. At least you haven't got a film that's worth watching.

An example of this story arc is *The Wizard of Oz*). Dorothy (*protagonist*) has to overcome the wicked witch (*her inner shadow*) by making friends with the scarecrow (*her mind*) the tin man (*her heart*) and the lion (*her courage*). She falls asleep in the poppy field (*her unconscious mind*) and discovers she already has the power to get herself back to Kansas (*by clicking her heels*). The power has been inside her all along. Boys movies do the same thing but with more sword fighting, swearing and car chases.

However, because a story has a beginning, a middle and an end, we imagine that our life is the same. We think our life is played out in linear time. If we have killed the wicked witch in Scene 2, we don't expect her to reappear in Scene 3. Similarly if we've forgiven the boy who lied to us at age 17, we don't expect those feelings of betrayal to resurface when we're 35.

It follows that if we have a moment of enlightenment that banishes depression, we need to develop some new skills, in order to prevent the exiled thing from sneaking back over the border. We have to work to stay at the higher frequency.

Discipline is not a word I am normally associated with, but it's a very important component of developing these skills. Our old behaviour and thought patterns are ingrained – neurons that fire together wire together. Every time we repeat a behaviour, the neural pathway gets stronger. But the good news is, these fused neurons can be un-fused and left to wither on the vine, and new neural pathways can be developed to take their place. However, the new behaviour has to be repeated often enough to turn into a habit if we're going to do a successful rewiring job.

I'm going to list the best tools for developing these skills in the last section, but first a brief look at time (for people who can't get their head around the Stephen Hawking version).

Life is exasperating because we live in two worlds. Our body lives in the third dimension, where linear time exists (we are born, we grow up, we die... and always in that order!).

The fourth dimension is Time. Our spirit lives in the fifth dimension and beyond, outside the construct of time and space (the structures by which we hold things together in the "real" world).

Once we get past the third dimension, linear time does not exist, only the present moment does. This means that we are living the ENTIRE STORY... ALL THE TIME. While we are here, we constantly have to fight our compulsions, question what kind of reality we're buying into and learn to make different choices. More love. Less fear.

In the energy world, we don't move forwards, in a linear fashion, we expand so that we can contain more. Our spirit always wants to be "more" (Obviously without a connection to our spirit, we interpret this impulse in the world of form – more cake, more drama, more success).

There is no cosmic "to do list" where things get ticked off and STAY ticked off, before we move on to the next thing. There is no goal, no finish line, no completion. Our spirit is a *process*, not a *thing* with a beginning, middle and end. It's a process of CONSTANTLY BECOMING.

Think of a waterfall. A glass of water is a *thing*, but a waterfall is a *process*. The atoms in the glass of water remain the same, but the water in the waterfall is never the same from one second to the next. It's a constant process, of becoming something else... while at the same time remaining the same thing (a waterfall).

We are simultaneously a thing (the body) and a process (the spirit). And we can focus our attention on either aspect of ourselves.

In the same way that a glass of water is fairly uninteresting, our bodies have a very limited range. Our spirit, on the other hand is extraordinary – just like a waterfall.

183

1 It's practical – it can mould and shape things, move debris out of the way, and provide sustainable energy.

2 It's beautiful – you could almost use the word awesome to describe it.

When we look at this "living in the NOW" business from the perspective of our body, it's exasperating, because we want the "beginning, middle and end" story. We hate the feeling of being incomplete, and the prospect of never finishing. We stay up late to empty the in box on the computer, and go to bed happy. But when we wake in the morning, it's filled up again. This is what life is like these days.

So rather than fighting the exasperation of...

1 Feeling incomplete.

2 Never finishing.

It's far better to embrace both of them. Be happy with feeling incomplete and never finishing. LOVE the process of becoming without any need attached. Create, not for the joy of completion or the satisfaction of accomplishing something, but for the sheer pleasure of creating. This feminine philosophy (pleasure!) doesn't sit well with the mind and its endless to do lists, so it takes some getting used to. Living in peace with this process, allows us to expand our capacity to contain more energy. And the more energy we can contain, the higher the frequency we can live at.

We still want the masculine counterpart to this (achieving goals). It's about balance, not swinging from one side to the other, because when we're balanced we choose different goals.

If we want to achieve a goal, we like to know what that goal looks like. This is a problem if the goal is "being happy". How do you create an image of that? Smiling people don't work – they can make you want to punch a hole through your computer screen. When you're depressed, images of people running along a beach trailing a scarf #asgoodasitgets or drinking cocktails with party hats on #sohilarious make things worse, because if you superimpose yourself into the picture you'd probably want to die. This makes you believe that you actually don't have any talent for happiness BUT THIS IS NOT TRUE. Happiness, like love, doesn't translate well into images or words.

Imagine if we (as a collective species) had to make the leap from a lower to a higher state of consciousness. How would we do this? In the lower frequency, the power source we rely on is adrenaline. Adrenaline is created by fear. Fear gives us the motivation to survive, compete and win.

But if we want to get to the higher frequencies of joy, love and creativity, we need a different kind of energy, and perhaps we have to be dismantled in order to allow this new energy in.

I know I have been given a temporary reprieve from depression in order to create a better strategy for dealing with it. I have been shown what it is like to live outside of the prison of the mind so that I can create a new blueprint. I know where I want to go now. Those other goals I had – status, security, popularity seem two dimensional, like a house of cards, just waiting to be collapsed.

Once you know where you're going, it's easier to get there. But it still takes a lot of discipline to change the old beliefs every moment, IN THE NOW. There is no quick fix that allows us to leap from here to the fifth dimension (apart from death of course). Our mission (should we choose to accept it) is to bring the fifth dimension here.

We're gonna need a smaller mustard seed!

TWENTY EIGHT

Building a Platform
on Flatland

One more thing before we get onto tools and techniques to build the platform.

If the boundary between the third and fifth dimension is the construct of "time and space", and we've looked at "time", it might be helpful to take a brief look at "space".

In the 17th century, Edwin Abbott, a mathematician/satirist (now there's a balanced mind!) wrote a novella called *Flatland*, in which he satirised the narrow minded thinkers of Victorian England. I'll borrow from Tom Kenyon's précis of it.

Flatland, as it's title suggests, is a two dimensional world. The inhabitants of Flatland are like paper cut outs of geometric shapes. They see everything as lines, circles and triangles. They are convinced that everything is flat, because they have no other frame of reference. One day a sphere passes through their world – this is a 3D shape passing through a 2D world.

From their perspective, the sphere first appears as a point. The point then expands into a circle. The circle becomes larger until it reaches the largest diameter of the sphere, then mysteriously it gets smaller, and smaller, returns to a point and disappears.

Everyone in Flatland has a different opinion about this strange phenomena! – academics, conspiracy theorists, scientists, religious people. Some of them focus their attention on the small point, others think the big circle is more significant.

But, everyone is deluded. Because no-one in a two dimensional world can conceive of a three dimensional reality.

We are living in a three dimensional version of the Flatland story, trying to interpret the fifth dimension with our very limited minds. Physicists have one view, mystics have another. The mystics have actually been there, but struggle to describe it without a frame of reference.

The good news for evolution, is that scientists have discovered we have huge amounts of DNA lying dormant. Because it's inactive they labelled it "junk DNA" but perhaps it's just DNA that's waiting to be activated, once we raise our level of consciousness. It's obvious that we would have to do the consciousness raising bit first, because if we had access to the power of the fifth dimension while remaining at a low frequency we'd create an even worse mess than the one we've made already.

All the systems we currently live in are designed to keep us stupid and disconnected, so that we don't make this necessary leap in consciousness. Corporations sell us food that clogs our brains, drugs that numb us and media that dumbs us down and keeps us distracted from the real issues. They get very rich doing this, and they get to survive, because if we were actively engaged it would be very easy to change the world. After all, there are 99% of us and 1% of them.

Corporations are the devil.

Scientists have recently developed some new drugs that are real money spinners. They say they are just responding to market forces, like this is a good thing. People are unhappy, so they want to eat junk food. Rather than deal with the unhappiness, Big Pharma have developed a drug you can take so that you can eat and not gain weight.

A section of the gay community indulge in chemical sex. They get high on a cocktail of drugs, lose inhibitions and judgment and have unprotected sex with a variety of partners all weekend. In response to this, Big Pharma are now selling a drug that enables them to have unprotected sex without contracting HIV.

This is a world gone mad and conjures a picture of a future generation whose lives are reduced to eating and orgasms while hooked up to a virtual reality of social media. Yes, emotional pain is tough, but accountability trumps anaesthetic. We need to break the spells corporations cast to keep everyone dumbed down.

Though scientists and mystics vary on their interpretation of the fifth dimension, there is one thing they agree on. Once you step outside time and space to the fifth dimension, you have the ability to affect time and space in creative ways that are not available to you from the 3rd dimension. This includes the spontaneous healing of illnesses (sometimes called miracles); solutions for complex problems (usually called genius ideas); and serendipitous events (massive good luck). So, apart from an antidote to depression, there are lots of bonus reasons for expanding our consciousness to this higher level.

It's not easy of course – reaching towards somewhere that we can't visualise or describe. We have conflicting loyalties. Our bodies are firmly rooted in time and space but our consciousness can travel beyond it. Our bodies like to cling, but limiting our consciousness to a three dimensional reality is a bit like trapping a bird in a cage, or an animal in a zoo. We lose our ability to give full expression to who we are. We become miserable creatures staring at the rails, waiting for someone to appear with a bucket of chicken.

In terms of perception, the world is about to go through the biggest change in its history, so it's helpful to look at the impact of one of the last big changes – the invention of telescopes and microscopes. These two instruments completely changed our perception of the world, and our subsequent reality.

Telescopes – Before their invention, we thought that the world was flat, and the sun revolved around us. We only trusted the real world, and real was limited to what our eyes could see. The first astronomer who stated otherwise, was locked up for being insane.

Microscopes – Before their invention, we thought the smallest thing in the world was an ant. Doctors did surgery on people with unwashed knives and wondered why their patients were dying. The doctor who suggested germs were killing them (in other words invisible things!) was also locked up for being insane.

Now we are moving into the energy age, we have to learn to trust things we can't see at a whole new level. We certainly need a better way to manage energy if we're going to avoid medicating half the world. Because things are only going to get faster and more chaotic.

My depression lasted about three months and my recovery from depression probably lasted about three more. I didn't write this book in real time as a journal, or by now you'd have died of boredom. I condensed things to avoid repetition. I did lots of workshops and Ayahuasca experiences. They didn't take place over one weekend, but over many weekends.

During that time I tried different things, which I'll document here, in the hope that this will help others. The strategies aren't just cognitive, they cover all the bases – mind, body, emotions and spirit.

If we're going to climb to a higher level, we need a platform, and platforms usually have four pillars, because that makes them more stable. Doing just one thing (for example mindfulness) doesn't work because doing one thing is like climbing a ladder, not building a platform on Flatland.

I've fallen off a lot of ladders, because I'm gullible and highly susceptible to marketing. Also, I'm a high achiever who's lived on adrenaline all my life, so I LOVE running up ladders. But I'd recommend a different approach now. Building something (like a platform) doesn't sound so glamorous, but in the end, it will save lots of time and money.

A four pronged approach is better, not just because it creates a stronger foundation (so no falling down) but because it creates a stronger force for upward momentum, to the place where real happiness lives.

The mind can be part of the team, but it doesn't get to run the show. We have a second "brain" in the heart, and we have a third "brain" in the gut, so the emotions and the body play an equally big part. Finally we have a fourth "brain" just outside the body.

A team with four key players can tackle depression, as long as they're all on the same side. Because only a strong unified force, can defeat the gravitational pull of a black hole.

PART TWO

The Tools

TWENTY NINE

Pillar One – The Body

**Tools to Strengthen the First Pillar
– Diet and Exercise**

In the fight against depression, a healthy physiology is a tremendous asset. This is a tricky situation because when we're depressed, probably the LAST thing we want to do is eat a healthy diet or do any exercise.

Depressed people want two things – energy and comfort. Energy to get through the day – because let's face it we have zero motivation. And comfort to soothe the despair – because the joy of achievement is a far distant memory.

Energy

There are two forms of energy that we can use to drive ourselves...

Low frequency fuel – adrenaline

High frequency fuel – creativity

When we're depressed, we're running at such a low frequency, that either...

1 We can't even get stressed enough to produce adrenaline. For example, the fear of losing a job provides enough adrenaline for the normal person to get out of bed in the morning. But life feels so unreal for the depressed person that a reasonable response to this scenario could be something like #Whatever.

Or...

2 We've been running on stress for so long that we have adrenal fatigue. This is the body's way of shutting up shop and leaving a sign on the door. Burn out. No adrenaline available until further notice.

If we can't create energy through stress, then the only remaining option for creating energy is sugar – either in food, or alcohol. This is one of the reasons why it's so hard to give up. It's practically keeping us alive.

The only way I've found to resolve this energy conundrum, is to leapfrog over adrenaline to creativity. Turning the depression into a creative act has saved a lot of people from cutting off parts of their anatomy in the middle of a dark night. Obviously this is not 100% foolproof, and some artists don't make it through till morning, which is why we need support from the other pillars.

Find something that you can turn into a creative pursuit – drawing, journaling, cooking, flower arranging or anything else you can think of.

Comfort

"I'm really depressed, I want some raw carrots!" said no depressed person EVER. There's a biological reason why we crave sugar – it lights up the pleasure centres in the brain. Our bodies are hard wired for it. Thousands of years ago, sugar was in short supply (the odd strawberry if weather was warm) and because sugar provides such a fast energy boost, Mother Nature made sure we'd love it. It's fair to say that she didn't foresee the wonders of technology (a vending machine wherever humans pause for longer than two seconds) nor did she anticipate the ways we would use our creativity (50 shades of cup cakes).

Some years ago (rubbish at dates) Anthony Sclafani, Professor of Psychology, needed some fat rats for a study he was doing. He tried to get the rats to put on weight by adding some extra fat to their food, but they wouldn't eat more than they needed, so this didn't work. After trying various foods he put out chocolate bars and sweetened milk and the rats went crazy for it. They couldn't stop eating and quickly grew obese. Their craving over rode the normal biological brakes of the body.

Job done, you could say. But this piqued his curiosity so he did a further experiment in which the rats would get a nasty electrical shock if they tried to get the sweet food. Sure enough, they still went for it. Rather than eat the other food that was easily available... they increased their tolerance for pain.

Food corporations realised this was a licence to print money, so they proceeded to add sugar to every food they sold... bread, soup, health drinks. In Paleolithic times we ate no sugar, in the 1700s we ate about 5lbs a year, but now we eat a staggering 152 lbs a year. Mass marketing. Corporations aren't fat cats, they're rich cats... with fat mice.

I say all this to help the people who struggle with an addictive personality... because IT'S NOT YOUR FAULT. The dice are stacked against you.

On the other hand, we really do need to find a way to cut out the sugar because IT MAKES DEPRESSION A WHOLE LOT WORSE. This isn't the place to go into the science, because I'm writing an overview. Entire books have been written on the subject, (like *Sugar Blues* and *Pure White and Deadly*) so if you're interested in the science, Amazon is close at hand. Suffice to say, sugar and depression are a match made in hell.

The next most helpful thing to give up or cut down on is grains. (Best book on this subject is *Grain Brain*). Basically a diet that's carb heavy causes inflammation in the body. This has been common knowledge when treating things like arthritis, but inflammation isn't restricted to our joints, it also affects the brain. Inflammation in the brain makes depression much, much worse. Human evolution has been going on for over two million years, but it's only in the last 10,000 years that we added small amounts of grain to our diet. And it's only in the blink of an eye (in evolutionary terms) that we've added MASSIVE amounts of wheat.

Again, you can blame the food corporations who noted how busy our lives had become and therefore our need for food that can be consumed while we are on our way from place to place. In cities, it's difficult to find a street that doesn't have a café and pretty much everything they sell is made out of wheat. The bonus ball for the food corporations was the discovery of "mouth feel." If a cup of coffee is looking for its perfect partner, an apple (even in its wildest dreams) can't compete with a croissant.

The apple will never be chosen, unless it has a Fairy Godmother, with her wand of wheat, to transform it into a Danish pastry.

Most supermarkets now have a bakery section. Marketing companies know that the smell of baked bread and croissants is a huge magnet, because it gives the supermarket a "homely" feel. But all the dough they use comes from a single source, shipped overnight from huge warehouses (not so homely!) Scientists have invented new kinds of fast growing wheat (with 20 times the normal amount of gluten) and new kinds of fast acting yeast. Food companies don't want to sit around for half an hour waiting for the dough to rise in the normal way, because "time is money." These two short cuts have produced baked goods that are a million miles from those of previous generations. They practically turn into glue in our intestines.

Fat, on the other hand is good news for the brain. Good fats obviously, the kind you see stacked high in Whole Foods. Almond Butter. Coconut oil, Avocados. But even butter from the corner shop is good and is now considered a health food (yay!) Though probably not on a big wedge of toast (boo!) It turns out that the medium chain triglycerides found in fat, are what our brains have been CRAVING and if we stack up on these, the craving for sugar decreases enormously, and our brain fog disappears.

Diet

In my non scientific research (so check for yourself) the best diets to treat depression are juicing (which is the fastest and easiest way to get masses of vegetables into your system), the Paleo diet (high fat/protein and greens) and the alkaline diet (everything green plus good fat). Greens and fat are majorly important. If you get up in the morning and there's no food in the fridge, put a blob of butter in a cup of coffee and whizz it up in a blender. This will save you from running the gauntlet of the pain au chocolats on the way to the train station.

You can't go wrong with vegetables and fruit (though the ratio should be stacked mostly vegetable not mostly fruit!) There's a free video by Jason Vale called *Super Juice Me* in which he cured 8 people of 22 diseases by putting them on a juice diet for 30 days. Greens are key because they photosynthesise, so you're practically eating light to dispel the darkness! There is SO much on the internet about Paleo diets that it's hard to single anything out.

The easiest method for knowing what to eat is to look at the ingredients. This way you'll know you're eating real food rather than food made by people in white coats. Butter for instance says "butter". On the other hand, the ingredients for low fat spread sound like a chemistry experiment. The ingredients for biscuits have to be written in small font or they wouldn't fit on the package.

Everyone has to find their own way through sugar or alcohol addiction, because we're all different. Some people find a strategy of moderation works. Magazines promote diets that have healthy meals and include a mid afternoon "treat" of a two bar Kit Kat to curb sugar cravings. This is a ridiculous idea for people like me. A two bar Kit Kat is an amouse bouche, a wake up call to the taste buds who immediately clamour for a family sized bar of Green and Blacks.

When I did the Ayahuasca ceremony, I gave up sugar for seven days. Having a specific reason to give up sugar helps. Magazines are full of people who are on diets because they want to look good on their wedding day or they want a bikini body to flaunt on the beach. But when you're in a full blown depression, it's unlikely anyone is going to want to marry you any time soon, and the last thing you feel like doing is joining the happy crowd for a game of volleyball in a swimsuit.

Having to give up for the Ayahuasca ceremony was a great incentive. If you're going to invest time, energy and money in something, you want it to work. Seven days is enough to get through all the physical cravings, so after that it's easier to keep going.

Unless you're an idiot like me.

I kept going for another few days. I was feeling really good, so went out to dinner with a friend. A friend who happened to say at the end of the meal. "Can I see the dessert menu?"

I should have known better. I should have run for the hills. Instead the saboteur voice in my head said. "It's just one little dessert. You're fine with the sugar thing now. In fact you're NORMAL, just like this person sitting opposite you."

Fast forward a couple of hours. My friend is now at home, no doubt drinking a camomile tea and reading a book whereas I am walking the streets like a crazy person looking for my next fix. Within two days, my sugar consumption was back to its pre Ayahuasca levels.

You are the only person who can figure out what strategy works for you. But be honest with yourself. There are no judgments here, just massive amounts of compassion.

Exercise

Apart from changing your diet, the other great tool for strengthening the Body Pillar is exercise. Any exercise will do as long as it gets your heart rate up. Walking, running, rowing, dancing. Again, there are loads of books on the science of exercise, I'm just going to state the three benefits as far as they relate to depression.

1 Doing something every day (that you don't particularly want to do) trains the body in a "deferred gratification" kind of way. Consistency sends a signal to the body which says "we're serious this time." A depressed body doesn't want to do exercise because it has no energy, but paradoxically exercise creates energy. After a few weeks it gets easier. As with sugar or alcohol, tell yourself it's only for a few weeks, and then keep going.

2 Exercise creates endorphins which make you feel good. Because you may no longer be getting feel good sensations from your addiction of choice, you need something to replace them with. Endorphins help. Many people have found that exercise has been more helpful than anti-depressant medication in their battle against depression. Scientific studies have backed this up so don't take my word for it. Exercise also helps with anxiety because it's rhythmic which is very calming.

3 Exercise gets oxygen into the body, which is good for lots of reasons. Most of us have developed bad habits of shallow breathing. This alone affects our physiology. If we only use a small part

of our lungs, our shoulders start to round forward. We slump. Even the word fits with depression – to fall, sink or collapse. Changing our physiology by breathing more deeply and expanding the lungs, sends a message that says "yes" to life. Breath is the interface between us and the outside world. The way we breathe therefore is an important communication. Either we're allowing life in, or we're disallowing it.

Each of the four pillars, though separate, interact with each other.

The place where the Body interacts with the Mind is through breathing – yoga is a good discipline that links Body and Mind through the breath. People who have a good relationship with their mind, (an obedient mind!) love to do Meditation, but people (myself included) who have a chaotic mind, find physical exertion is a better way to stop the mind's endless chatter.

The place where the body interacts with the Emotions is also through breathing... so that's where we're going next.

THIRTY

Pillar Two – The Emotions

**Tools to Strengthen the Second Pillar
– Breathing and Sound**

Emotion of course is energy in motion. If we're depressed, we desperately need energy, so this section is crucial. Humans are designed to feel things through their emotional system. If we weren't able to feel, life would be purely functional. The intelligence that created us, clearly meant us to enjoy the experience of being on this planet, otherwise we would be walking around like R2-D2. A brain in a tin can.

We create other humans because it's enjoyable watching them learn, grow and discover new things for themselves. The intelligence that created us probably feels the same way. It is impossible to learn, grow and discover without a guidance system in place. That guidance system is the emotions. Our emotions tell us what we are thinking. This is a great system because we are not aware of most of our thoughts. If we feel bad, we're thinking negative thoughts, so now we're aware of them, we can change them, before deciding what to do next. It's a fool-proof system.

But it's not human proof.

If we're feeling anxious about lack of money, we think we need to change something in the outside world – borrow money, change our job, invest in the stock market. These are fear driven reactions to the anxiety we feel inside. But the stimulus didn't come from the outside world, it came from our thoughts. Our imagination tells us how bad things are going to be if we can't pay the mortgage, or we lose our job or the credit cards are cancelled. None of these are happening anywhere except in our head.

If, on the other hand, we check out what we're thinking when we feel anxious, there's a different response. We stop the crazy (completely unhelpful) thoughts, get balanced, and then we can choose a response. This isn't a fear driven response, it's usually a much more creative one.

Most of us think our emotions are generated in response to the outside world, but they're not. They're completely generated in response to our thoughts about what is going on in the outside world. Our emotions allow us to know what we're thinking, so we can shake this out and start again with better thinking.

If animals feel something they don't like (e.g. anger or fear) they move it out of their system very quickly. Eckhart Tolle's example cites ducks on a pond. A duck gets into a fight with another duck over a piece of bread, then once they move away, they shake their wing feathers furiously. This moves the energy out of their body, so that five minutes later when they circle the pond and meet the same duck, all the animosity is gone. It's like it never happened.

We hold onto resentment for years. In the same way that humans learnt to over ride their biological system, (see Pillar One) they also learnt to over ride their emotional one. They called it "becoming civilised," which is a fancy phrase for feeling one thing, while doing another.

If someone treats us unfairly, instead of being angry, we shove down the feeling, say nothing and plot ways of getting revenge later on. Emotions are supposed to be a "present moment" guidance system. They are like waves of energy that move through us. In a functioning system, they bring information, and then they leave. But we trap them in our body. Once trapped they create a magnetic charge. And then life becomes really complicated.

We can't see electricity, and similarly we can't see these magnetic pockets of energy in the body. The only way to identify them is through the charge they create. Here's an example. Somebody I knew was struggling through a divorce. She was sitting in front of me extremely stressed, because she didn't have the money to pay her child's school fees.

I felt really uncomfortable.

"Of course you feel uncomfortable" the mind says, "because you're such a wonderful empathic, kind human being."

This isn't true. It was my trapped emotions that were being triggered – the feelings I had shoved down on the way to becoming an adult. All those times when I felt helpless, when I was scared of having no money, created feelings that I'd squashed down and stored in my body. Now they were sending out little electro magnetic signals, which had pulled in someone who was a perfect match on the outside to what I was feeling on the inside.

I didn't feel uncomfortable because of her, but because of me.

This should have been an opportunity to really feel those feelings, and question my thoughts, so that I could let them go. Did I choose to do this?

Are you crazy!

Fast as lightening I whipped out my cheque book to lend her the money. This solved the pain problem, and shoved the feelings back down where they belonged.

A couple of years later (when the money had not been returned) I saw her in an expensive restaurant. I felt furious (though of course being a civilized human said nothing) and went home to shove the feelings of anger on top of the feelings of victimhood. Obviously there was quite a crowd gathering down there. Almost a party, which is why flares were sent up with urgent requests for pizza and ice cream.

Corporations rely on our faulty inner systems in order to manipulate us into behaviour that suits them (as opposed to behaviour that can heal us). The sole purpose of media and advertising agencies is to make us feel an emotion...

1 An emotion we WANT to feel, like happiness (buy this phone it will bring you joy), or pride (buy this face cream, it will make you look years younger).

2 An emotion we DON'T want to feel, like guilt (buy this kid's toy, you've been working late all week), or fear (buy this face cream, you're looking really old).

If we don't want to be scared little mice at the mercy of fat cat corporations, who have turned us into rampant consumers, we need to take back control of our emotional system.

More importantly (for this is a book about depression) if we want to be able to fully engage with life, we need confidence in our ability to deal with emotions. There is a correlation between creative people and depression. Creativity requires openness to events, images and information, which trigger emotions, that can be expressed in works of art. Unexpressed, these emotions can turn inwards and pull us down.

Love, anger and despair can create art that moves us, because there's movement (emotion) in the original rendering of it. Adele channelled her heartbreak and depression into an album, which brought joy and comfort to many people, sold 30 million copies and won a Grammy.

If we are going to turn our depression into something creative and useful, then an ability to feel and navigate emotions is key.

Breathing

The interface between the energy in the body and the energy in the outside world, is the breath. Obviously. If we stop breathing we die. When we feel a strong emotion, like fear, the first thing we do is hold our breath. This effectively traps the emotion in the body, presumably so we can let it out later, once the danger is passed. But we never go back to release it.

There are Breathing workshops specifically designed to locate and free these trapped emotions. These are a bit homeopathic in nature – treating like with like. The breath traps the emotion, so an even bigger breath can release it. Normal breathing (unconscious and shallow) won't do the trick, it needs to be conscious and deep. This takes a bit of getting used to. The body creates resistance – dizziness in the head, dryness in the mouth, tiredness in the lungs.

Yoga is great for increasing conscious breath control. There are various forms of yogic breathing. You could start by simple rhythmic breathing – breathing in and out slowly and evenly. There's counting the breath – breathe in for 4 counts, hold for 4 counts, breathe out for 4 counts, hold for 4 counts, repeat. There's alternate nostril breathing – holding a finger against the left nostril, breathe in through the right nostril, switch the finger to the other side and breathe out through the left nostril, in through the left nostril, switch the finger, out through the right nostril. Repeat for five to ten minutes. This breathing has the added benefit of balancing the left and right hemispheres of the brain, which helps enormously with creativity.

Recently some people have tried to turn yoga into a personal brand. Hot bikram yoga is run by a sociopath who purports to own intellectual property rights on body positions that have been in existence for thousands of years. If Indian villagers knew the price yoga pants would sell for in Lulu Lemon, there would have been a mass exodus from the rice fields years ago.

Opportunists get in everywhere with their one stop strategy of turning a good thing into a marketing opportunity. The practice of Yoga (for it is a practice, not an occasional event) has been around since the 6th century BC. The word yoga means to join or to unite. We unite mind, body and spirit, through the breath, to reach the ultimate goal, which is freedom or liberation from the lower frequencies of energy that drag us down. It's not an exercise class to tone your upper arms, make you more bendy, and show off your Sweaty Betty tank top, it's a way of overcoming resistance.

Depression is resistance to life. And the only thing that overcomes resistance is practice and discipline. Don't be put off by the identity of yoga and breathing workshops, trust your intuition and you'll find what works for you.

Sound

Music and emotions go so well together! Trapped emotions can be processed through sound. If we feel heartbroken and need a good cry, sad songs do the trick. If we feel weak, a power ballad can lift us up. If we feel anxious, classical music can calm us down. In a movie theatre, sound is a huge component in helping us feel every emotion from extreme joy to extreme fear. Think of the soundtrack to *Jaws* – we were more scared by the music than the big plastic shark.

In the same way that a sad song can trigger and release feelings of heartbreak, there are certain sounds that can trigger and release deep seated feelings of fear and isolation. Our survival fears are pre-verbal. Most of these emotions were trapped before we learnt to talk, so songs with words are not appropriate. Very deep and very rhythmic sounds are. Sounds that have more of a low frequency vibration, a resonance rather than an actual tune.

This is why sound healing (which I experienced in both the breathing workshop and the Ayahuasca ceremony) often uses instruments like bass drums, didgeridoos and jaw harps to get the required effect. The negative "thought pattern" that I needed to release – the feeling of not wanting to be here – could have happened around the time of my birth. You can't get to this through a cognitive process. Your cognitive brain hasn't even been formed yet.

I also experienced higher frequency sounds in the workshops. These sounds help us access the right hemisphere of the brain. We already have access to the left, which interprets the world through language, but language often hinders our attempts to access the right side – which is the portal to connected consciousness. Listening to certain pure sounds is a way of activating the non-language based hemisphere of the right brain. There are lots of examples of this more "spiritual" music on the internet.

A good way to strengthen the connection between body and emotions is running to a curated soundtrack. Start with primal base sounds to shake out the emotions of fear and anger, move to soaring songs that build power in the solar plexus, passionate songs that engage the heart and finish with sacred sounds, like Indian chanting music or Diva Premal for the cool down at the end.

There is a popular saying "The devil has all the best tunes". Perhaps it's time to create a new playlist.

THIRTY ONE

Pillar Three – The Mind

**Tools to Strengthen the Third Pillar
– Mindfulness, NLP/CBT and Other Initials**

Traditional medical models, tend to agree that depression is all in the mind. But to them the mind and the brain are inter changeable terms, so their treatments are restricted to medication for the brain. Health services are heavy, slow, bureaucratic machines that are run like corporations. There are no good words in THAT sentence.

The main treatments available are anti depressants, which increase serotonin levels in the brain. Depressed people don't have a lot of serotonin in their brain and therefore can't send "happy" information to the rest of the body. But cutting edge science has now discovered a couple of interesting things. We don't have one brain, or one Mission Control, we have three – one in the head, one in the heart and one in the gut. Information is not a one way street, from the brain to the body. First, there are far more messages travelling from the heart to the mind, rather than vice versa. Second, 80-90% of serotonin is found in the gut, not the brain, which is why diet is so important.

Kinesiology has made rapid progress in accessing the intelligence of the body. By testing the strength of the muscles, a practitioner can ascertain which foods the body needs/likes and which foods it reacts negatively to. Of course these preferences can change continually so it's more cost effective to develop the skill of interpreting for ourselves what the body is trying to say.

Kinesiology can also reveal negative beliefs. A friend of mine was able to discover one of these hidden beliefs using this method. When she said out loud "My best is good enough" her muscles tested weak as a kitten, signifying that this was definitely NOT what she believed. All her life she had been knocking herself out, trying to be better, trying to be perfect, trying to reach a goal that could never be attained. It's heart breaking what we do to ourselves, without even realising.

Important messages come from the body – and from the heart. It would be more intelligent to open these channels of communication instead of focussing all our attention on the brain.

When it comes to mental health, a fair amount of medical science is based on correlation. This is like finding out (in research) that 60% of people who suffer from depression like red cars, then going on to say that red cars cause depression. Advice from the medical world changes frequently – because it's wrong to begin with. Also there are huge sums of money involved, so statistics are always skewed in favour of the people who benefit from the research – the drug companies (who also happen to fund the research in the first place, so go figure).

Chemical medicine is a blunt instrument, because it can't allow for complexity. By the time you read this, things will have probably changed again. Science makes new discoveries all the time. What's important here is not the information, it's the willingness to be open to the fact that there are usually multiple facets to health problems and multiple facets to their cure.

I say this NOT to denigrate traditional medicine, just to help those people for whom the drugs don't work.

Mindfulness

Mindfulness is the buzz word of the moment. You can't move for mindfulness programs in the workplace, schools or spa resorts. Airports and railway stations are loaded with mindfulness books. This is quite a feat, considering the premise and practice of mindfulness could probably fit on one A4 sheet of paper. I shall therefore rise to the challenge, and attempt to do this for you.

Our mind is thinking all the time, but we are not conscious of most of these thoughts. THE MIND THINKS ALL BY ITSELF. This is a bit like becoming so used to having a radio on in the background that we forget about it and have no idea what programs it's actually broadcasting.

Try this little exercise – say to yourself "I wonder what I'm going to think of next?" and wait. You don't choose your thoughts consciously. They choose you.

We have a platform with four legs, but the mind is power crazy and wants to run the whole show, so it rises up above the other three. That's why we fall off.

We have to do something about this imbalance.

When things go wrong, and we have a negative feeling, like heartbreak, we presume this feeling is coming *from* our emotions. But the emotions didn't create it. Emotion is just an indicator of what we are already creating with our imagination. Thought precedes feeling. Whenever we think of something that happened in the past and feel sad, we are only suffering in our memory, not in real life.

Again, when we are fearful of something that might happen in the future, we are suffering in our imagination, not in real life.

The images in our head are not real, but we react as if they are.

In real life "bad" things happen once. In the life that our mind has constructed, they happen again, and again, and again. That betrayal. That stupid remark you made. That job you fucked up. They happen over and over and over again... probably even when you're asleep.

Over 90% of our thoughts, and a big percentage of our subsequent actions, are unconscious to us. We all know the feeling of "losing" whole wedges of time, for example when driving a car or completing a routine task at work. The way to counteract this is to become more aware.

Mindfulness seminars have various exercises to illustrate the above phenomena. You need exercises if you're going to stretch an A4 piece of paper into a two day event. I once sat through an exercise lasting 15 minutes involving a raisin. We had to look at the raisin, sense the raisin and what it had to say to us, remember raisin encounters we'd had in the past, smell the raisin, lick the raisin, play tongue tennis with the raisin, chew the raisin, swallow the raisin.

Of course I'd already swallowed the raisin 15 minutes earlier. I get it. I eat too fast and I get irritated by primary school teaching methods. If you're the same, save money, spend a few hours doing something – ANYTHING very slowly, while engaging your senses more fully.

After the exercise in slow "doing", move on to slow "thinking". This is trickier – particularly if you have a fast mind.

When we're depressed, we're unhappy, but we don't know why of course, because we're unconscious of our thoughts. The best way around this, is to do what Byron Katie calls "Inquiry". It means "capturing" all the unconscious thoughts. A blueprint for her work is freely available on the internet.

Think of a moment when you felt bad, then sit down with a piece of paper and identify all the thoughts you were thinking. Just grab all the thoughts and stick them on a piece of paper. These are the thoughts that are causing all the suffering, so they need interrogating. I'll do my situation as an example.

The event: My boyfriend doesn't want to be with me.

The thoughts: He should want to be with me. I'm sad he doesn't want to be with me. I'm angry that he left.

The reality: That's not a boyfriend in my head, it's an image. My boyfriend may not even be on the planet. I'm using an image to torture myself. My mind is out of control.

The learning: Everything in our world is a mirror. By changing a couple of words, we can reverse the mirror image so that it more accurately reflects the truth. For example. "He" should want to be with me becomes "I" should want to be with me. This is more accurate. I was an independent person who got sucked into his orbit by the sheer force of his magnetism. I left me. I'm angry that I left me. I'm sad that I don't want to be with me.

We have to learn to meet our own needs first – our need for love, security, value, connection – otherwise we tend to "leave ourselves" when we come into contact with anything that has a magnetic pull.

This is also true if we love status, food or shopping. We leave ourselves and turn the object of our attention into an addiction. We make bad decisions about what to buy, when to eat and how to work, because we're not "all there" anymore. There's nobody around, smart enough to make the good decisions.

This allows a bit of compassion in, and compassion is always a good thing. Quite often, the whole rush to find a soul mate in the outside world, is the mind sending us off in the wrong direction. We look outside instead of inside for the relationship that would bring us peace, joy and fulfilment.

The mind can create heaven or hell in every moment. But with discipline, we can regain mastery over the mind. As Byron Katie says, "just find the thought that kicks you out of heaven."

Our biggest addiction is our addiction to thought – in particular to the WAY we think. Depressed people think really bad thoughts about themselves. "I'm lazy. I'm hopeless. Why can't I be happy? Why can't I get out of bed? Why can't I be more like Patricia?" These thoughts have to stop.

For God's sake don't replace them with aphorisms from a new-age book. Your mind will throw them out, because they're not an accurate representation of how you actually feel. The mind will then ridicule you further for your attempts to believe something that's not true, and for the hideous phraseology (which to be honest is an accurate assessment – the mind isn't all bad, it's just a little unbalanced at the moment).

Retrain your mind to keep reaching for the slightly higher thought, the more loving thought but above all, the REALISTIC thought… "I'm in bed. It's difficult to get out of bed. That's all, no big deal. Just the facts, no judgment. When I'm ready to get out of bed I'll get out of bed. I'm not Patricia, I'm me. Somebody's got to be me, so it might as well be me. Apparently what being me involves in this moment, is hiding under a duvet. I love being me. I'm actually quite hilarious."

These thoughts are more likely to help you get out of bed with a smile. Punitive thoughts will just get you out of bed with a very bad attitude, and new age uber positive thoughts will get you out of bed feeling like a total fraud.

Anger, fear and sadness are by products of compulsive thinking. We need to overcome the compulsive thinking to get back in the flow.

Find the thought that kicks you out of heaven.

Simple. And difficult. But if it was easy, everyone would be doing it, instead of reading about it, which judging by the book sales is what people are actually doing.

NLP, CBT and Other Initials

These have fallen out of favour in recent times, since Mindfulness got its new corporate identity, modern branding and ubiquitous media campaign, but they're worth a mention because they come under the Mind section and have been around quite a long time now.

NLP is Neuro Linguistic Programming. Neuro is the brain. Linguistic is the language we use to talk to ourselves (and others), and programming is self explanatory – our mind runs on programs, but we can change these programs. NLP has various exercises to change the memory of an event. Some of these I described in the chapters about the first workshop. Notice the thoughts in your head, identify the story you're living by having these thoughts, and slowly start to re-write the script.

This doesn't happen overnight because thoughts can create an identity of their own. One thought is pretty harmless, but once it's been repeated often enough it forms an energetic clump. This becomes magnetic, thus drawing to it other similar thoughts – it can do this without your conscious awareness. The energy keeps growing, and pretty soon you've got something like an entity living inside you, taking advantage of free board and lodgings. That's when it develops a "voice" and appears to be a separate part of who you are – often a very vocal and opinionated part.

CBT is Cognitive Behavioural Therapy, and was actually designed to help with depression. It is similar to NLP but focuses more on the present day, than re-writing the past. It is, as its name suggests, a way to look at behaviour patterns in almost forensic detail, in order to create a plan to dismantle or improve these patterns, so that new behaviours can be adopted. It teaches ways to identify distressing thoughts and evaluate how realistic they are. When the distorted thinking is changed to realistic thinking, people feel better.

Both NLP and CBT are about changing habits and training the mind through developing better strategies and new neural pathways, so in a way these are about developing an upgraded mind for better performance. Some people (balanced people) have used these techniques to great success. Others look and sound a bit robotic. The clue is in the name – programming. Programming works, to make something more efficient, but it often lacks a key ingredient – soul.

Which is where we're going next.

THIRTY TWO

Pillar Four Preamble – The Dynamics of Desire and Devotion

For many people the terms spirit and soul are interchangeable. They're certainly in the same category but differ slightly and of course will be interpreted through the blunt instrument of words, so things get a little tricky from here on.

The first three pillars feel as if they are very much "of the body".

The **Body** itself – this is obviously the most solid thing.

The **Emotions** – have less density, but are felt in the body, particularly in the heart. Sadness for example can be felt in the heart and humiliation can be felt in the solar plexus.

The **Mind** – thoughts have a lot less density. They're ephemeral, fleeting and hard to pin down, which is why becoming more aware of them takes discipline.

We are now at the outer reaches of the body - the Spirit and Soul. The spirit is at the interface between the mind and the fifth dimension and the soul is at the interface between the heart and the fifth dimension. There is no interface for the body, which is just a vehicle we use to travel around the third dimension - it's too dense to make the transition to the fifth.

The spirit is our "higher" mind, the one that comes into play when we subdue the ego with all its personalities and voices. We can tell when we receive guidance from the spirit because it tends to be wise and frightening. WISE because it has ALL the data, not just the tiny amount that we can hold in our brain. FRIGHTENING because if you can't die, you tend to come up with a few ideas that will scare the pants off the small, safe, ego mind.

The soul is our "expanded" heart, the one Jesus wore on the outside of his shirt. It is ALL ENCOMPASSING, because it cares about more than just ME, it wants the best long term solution for the most amount of people – that's just how things roll in the fifth dimension. It's more inclusive. Where the human heart has love, the soul has divine love. Divine love isn't romance or sentimentality. It's more like high voltage grace.

In our "energy body" we contain a lot of empty space. Space through which energy expresses itself. At the higher levels, this energy is driven by love and at the lower levels it's driven by fear. If depression is overwhelming sadness and heaviness of life at ground zero, then an ability to climb higher is a great advantage, because it allows us to be a space through which love can express itself.

It's like moving from the basement to the penthouse. If we've only known life in a basement, our world view is restricted. After all, we can only see the legs of people walking past the window and a small piece of pavement. We have no idea what's going on. Our desires are limited to things that bring temporary relief from boredom. The view from the penthouse is different because we can see more, we see the way everything connects together. This tends to alter the things we desire.

We all have the wiring in place to desire something and go after it. When we're depressed we question our desires – perhaps they were the wrong desires (clearly in the case of alcohol, sugar and unavailable men that's a correct assumption). Rather than "fix" the faulty desire mechanism however, our mind tends to give up on the whole notion of desire altogether. We become listless and bored with ourselves. We lose the will to go after things.

Depression is thwarted desire.

In truth, not many of us actually know what we want, which can make us blindly follow the desires of other people. We want money because everyone else is accumulating it and we don't want to get left behind. We want success for the same reason.

We're also very unspecific at framing our desires. If we question why we want money, we might say "to buy a house". If we ask why, the response might be "to feel secure" in which case our real desire is to feel secure. Security of course can't be bought with money. Rich people are more insecure than anyone, if the bars on their houses are anything to judge by.

This is a faulty desire mechanism.

Many people think that if they really knew what they wanted to *have* in life, things would be a lot easier, and if they only knew what they wanted to *do* in life, they would be happy. Searching for one's unique purpose is becoming fashionable these days.

Unfortunately most of us search for our purpose with our mind, rather than our spirit. We don't want to hear from our spirit, in case it reveals that our purpose is to work in the local library and be nice to old ladies. We want a grand purpose that guarantees we will be the envy of all our friends.

We need to fix our faulty desire mechanism.

If the spirit is the higher frequency version of the mind, and the soul is the higher frequency version of the heart, then devotion is the higher frequency version of desire. Desiring something has an element of need, which is low frequency energy. Desire for food can easily become greed. Desire for a person could actually be lust. Desire for status leads to narcissism. Desire is tricky energy to manage.

Devotion on the other hand protects us from falling into these low frequency energies.

If we're devoted to food, we have a certain respect for it. This respect stops us from bingeing or "using" food to deal with an emotional state. You don't see foodies or chefs who are devoted to food walking down the road eating unconsciously. A.A. Gill, the food critic, was once asked for his "top tip" on the best diet to lose weight. (He eats for a living, yet manages to remain slim). His strategy? Always eat with a knife and fork. Simple, yet profound. Be more conscious when you eat. Give the food some respect.

If we're devoted to a person, we have something that there is no word for. There is respect of course, but this implies a certain detachment. We have respect for people if we place a high value on their qualities. Devotion doesn't require the other person to be a certain way in order to "earn" our respect. The closest many people come to devotion is being devoted to a deity. This has always been a strange concept for me. If God is so magnificent, why does he need our devotion? Why does he need us on our knees in prayer and worship?

He doesn't of course, that's just a mad interpretation. The devotion is not for him, it's for us. Devotion is the kind of love that changes the person who is doing the loving. It's a practice that allows the soul to bypass the mind. Our mind is very involved with desire. It loves desire because it gets to stay in charge of the process. It decides who to love, what the terms and conditions of the loving involve, and the current state on the balance sheet of give and take. Devotion is not logical, so the mind just can't go there.

"What d'you mean, give and give, love and love, where's the payback?" The payback isn't in the external world, it's in the internal one. The process of loving in this way, changes us on the inside. It softens and expands us so that we can actually experience the love, rather than watching it play out on the outside. Richard and Karen, who facilitated the Ayahuasca workshop, had this kind of love for each other, which is why they were able to give so much to the participants. They could give from overflow, not from lack, not from need, not from a desire to prove anything.

Finally, the desire for status. Why the desire for status? Why do we need to be successful in the eyes of the world? We are of course using status to feel better about ourselves. We need the love and admiration of the outside world because our inner world doesn't feel real to us. The truth is – it's actually the other way around. Only the inner world is real, which is why admiration from the outside never feels the way it should, and never fills the emptiness.

Rock and roll stars get to understand this quite quickly. Admiration of a few people increases to a few hundred, then a few thousand, then hundreds of thousands. But with a faulty desire mechanism, the deep inner need is never satisfied. Drugs and alcohol don't help. Nor does the reckless behaviour of throwing a television from the hotel window. Perhaps drugs and alcohol COMBINED with reckless behaviour will work? This can lead to driving down the motorway at high speed having consumed a bottle of tequila. I suppose it's one way to enter the fifth dimension. But what a waste for human potential. Imagine if Tim Berners Lee had done that... we wouldn't even have the internet!

To have any chance of lasting success, we need to choose devotion to service over desire for status. Of course this makes no sense to the Mind, but we're not working that pillar now. The spirit world is an upside down version of the mind, in the same way that the soul is an inside out version of the heart.

In the hierarchy of the mind, the higher up the ladder you go, the less you serve – it's all about being the boss, and enjoying the rewards of high status – consumer goods and designer lifestyle.

Even the word "serve" has connotations with "servant" which is the bottom rung of the ladder.

In the hierarchy of the spirit, the higher up you go, the more you serve, because the greater the joy. I knew this in principle, but it wasn't until the Ayahuasca ceremony that I had an experience of it. There was a man there who was assisting Richard and Karen. This meant he emptied and cleaned the buckets of black vomit. I couldn't imagine anything worse. But when I thanked him the following day he looked confused. As far as he was concerned this act of devotion – to assist someone in their healing – was an honour and a privilege. This man was not an out of work hippy. He had run successful companies, earned millions of pounds, won international sporting competitions, and yet he found his greatest joy in a humble, menial act of service.

At least he discovered that life is upside down while relatively young. How sad it would be to find this out in old age. If life resembles a movie, this would be like the final frame of The Godfather trilogy. Huge wealth, respect of the global mafia community, no friends, but above all, alone... with some very, very dark thoughts.

So onto the tools that will allow us into the high frequency realms of devotion.

THIRTY THREE

Pillar Four – The Spirit/Soul

Tools to Strengthen the Fourth Pillar
– Meditation and Creativity

In a sense, the Spirit/Soul doesn't need any tools so this pillar is all about strengthening the interface between the mind and the spirit via a Higher Mind and strengthening the interface between the heart and the soul via an Expanded Heart.

There is one tool for each.

Meditation helps us gain access to high voltage thought – the kind of genius thought that can understand and process complexity.

Creativity helps us contain high voltage energy, so that we can become a channel, allowing the energy to move through us and find expression in the world. This energy is loving, compassionate, creative, and often called Grace.

Meditation

Meditation is the golden ticket as far as winning the war against depression is concerned. It also has some amazing side effects – it reduces anxiety, increases wellbeing and improves the immune system. If that's not enough, recent experiments show that it can actually change our DNA.

People of a left-brain orientation find meditation very difficult to do. First of all, it doesn't make sense, and we like things that make sense. In the logical left-brain world, things improve after we DO something, not as a result of doing nothing!

The mind is like a computer. Sometimes when we have a problem with the computer, rather than trying to find the problem (waste of time with poor results) it's often best to close down the computer and reboot it. Then the problem seems to miraculously fix itself.

Meditation does the same thing for our mind.

We don't trust this miraculous property, because we like to be in charge. Therefore we downgrade the power of meditation to a kind of "Time Out" for adults. When things become heated or chaotic, we remove ourselves from the emotional charge. People say things like "I need to take a moment," But they do this so they can *think* about things.

This isn't meditation. Meditation is NOT thinking about things. Our thinking is sub standard and is what caused the problem in the first place. More thinking won't help. In terms of the computer analogy, this is just putting the lid down on the laptop, going to get a cup of coffee, then coming back to retackle the problem with added help from the caffeine.

Meditation is switching off our thinking, so that we stop adding to the problem. This allows high frequency thought to gain access to our mind. Genius thought is around us, all the time, but we are like constantly moving targets. We have to stop. Only then can it hit our bull's eye.

The excuse we give for not developing the skill of meditating is that we don't have time. Again this is like running a computer for years without ever doing a software update. I am very guilty of this. I'm always clicking the NOT NOW button on updates. I rarely close my computer down because I often have about twenty seven tabs open. Eventually my computer runs so slow and sticky that I get exasperated. This is when my ex boyfriend would give me one of those looks and say "when did you last update your software?" He knows this is a rhetorical question.

Meditation seems like nothing but it's the key to everything. How can something so simple, change not only our physiology, but also our complex genetic coding? We have to swop our 3rd dimension rules for those of the 5th dimension if we want to make sense of this.

Start now.

Here are some tips you may find helpful.

1 Aim low. I can't emphasise this enough. Don't expect to be able to meditate for half an hour and feel like a failure when your mind wanders after 30 seconds. Instead start with one minute a day and then slowly increase.

2 Consistency is more important than quantity. It's not the one minute, it's the one minute EVERY day that's important. It sends a message to your mind that you're serious this time. Eventually the mind realizes this and stops finding excuses.

3 Find a way that works. This might be picking a mantra – a word or phrase that you repeat, to keep the other thoughts out. It might be observing the rise and fall of your breath. It might be staring at the flame of a candle, while it dances. It might be listening for sounds, without interpreting or narrating what the sounds are, in other words hearing the sound in your body, not your mind.

4 Breathe slowly and consistently. Try keeping to the same rhythm, for example 4 seconds for the in breath 4 seconds hold 4 seconds for the outbreath 4 seconds hold.

5 Turn it into a habit, like brushing your teeth. There's a lot less resistance in a habit, because you do it without thinking.

6 Find a location that works for you. Meditation doesn't have to happen sitting on a cushion. You can do walking meditation, shaking meditation, yoga meditation, dancing meditation, tai chi meditation.

Meditation/Creativity Crossover

Meditation teaches us to still the mind, and this pause allows us to take the needy edge off desire and turn it into devotion. Another thing that's helpful is to engage in dozens of daily "mini" pauses.

Eating lunch? Pause, and eat more consciously. Perhaps pretend you're a food critic and are going to have to give an account of what you ate. This will increase your sensory awareness.

Having sex? Pause to notice if you're in the experience or you're watching yourself in the experience. The ultimate high is to make love with the spirit, as well as the body, because you can run far more energy through the spirit. Connecting the spirit to the body requires getting the mind out of the way. Certain religions (not the patriarchal ones obviously) revere sex as an act of devotion to God. Sexual energy is highly creative because it comes from the same energy centre (second chakra). Puritan cultures produce very little creativity.

Working? Pause and connect to the aspect of the job that serves. Someone, somewhere will be benefiting from whatever you are doing. Focus on them, rather than on the data you're compiling or the thing you're fixing. When you serve humanity, humanity serves you right back. This is completely bonkers to the mind, so it's something that has to be experienced. Remember serving human-ity doesn't have to be big and epic (that's an ego trap). You don't have to find the cure for cancer, sometimes you just have to smile at people.

Creativity

When desire becomes devotion, we allow ourselves to become more open to the creative force. We've all seen evidence of desire that becomes obsession or compulsion. Murderous spurned lovers or religious fanatics are extreme examples. This makes us wary and closed off to the creative force. Devotion makes desire safe.

Being creative is a bit like androgynous baby making. There's the seed of an idea, (the masculine part) and the incubation/nurturing of the idea (the feminine part).

Tools for the masculine part – Meditation empties our monkey mind, with its endless repetitive thoughts and allows us to be "inspired" by a BRAND NEW idea. The word inspire comes from "in spirit" – it's just a higher frequency thought.

Tools for the feminine part – Creativity allows us to develop a better relationship with energy. If we have trust in our ability to contain energy, we are less likely to fight it or withdraw from it. This allows us to birth a fully realised idea, instead of a half formed mess.

Creativity also allows us to develop a better relationship with space. If we don't have a good relationship with empty space, we can feel lost – either in the void of depression or the chaos of madness.

Creativity Is All about the Relationship

In art, it's the relationship between shapes and colours and the empty space between them that creates the aesthetic beauty. In music, it's the relationship between the notes, and the pauses between the notes that give music its emotional power. In writing, it's the relationship between the words and the context that create meaning. Words without context are meaningless.

We are here to learn how to manage energy so that we can vessel greater amounts of power. We do this by moving forwards (even though we're scared) while at the same time continually letting go (even though we want to attach to things SO badly). We hold the space between how things are now and how we want them to be.

Most people give up on creativity because they can't hold this space – they are frustrated by their early creative efforts. They say "I'm not good enough" instead of saying "I'm not good enough... YET, but I can hold this space between now and future now, between what I have and what I want."

We don't run away from the space, and we don't fill it up with alternative stuff – like food, alcohol, social media or shopping. We have to BELIEVE that it's possible to just BE... without having something to avoid or something to crave. We empty ourselves out. In this way we become better conductors of the energy.

I found my creative practice in drawing, but creativity is an expression, not a narrow definition. Creativity and writing is about playing, loving, and above all ENJOYING THE PROCESS, rather than focussing on any end goal. You can try flower arranging, dancing, making up stories, dressing up. And if you can't find anything, then just say "yes". Each day, decide to say yes to whatever comes along.

In improvisational theatre, you have to say "yes" to keep the ball rolling. You respond and build on what the previous person said, no matter what they say. The minute you say "no" or "hang on a minute, that can't be right" the creativity stops, because the other person has nothing to respond to. Patricia Madson writes about this in *Improv Wisdom – Don't Prepare, Just Show Up*. Decide to live an unscripted life. Develop the confidence to know you can make things up as you go along. This is perfect practice for living in the now.

It makes sense to develop this skill, because if we have a script in mind, we can't anticipate the other person's response, so all our preparation goes to waste. This reminds me of the beginning of this book, where I prepared a wonderful script for the reunion with my ex boyfriend – which was of course a disaster. If we have a script in mind and it doesn't go to plan, our desire to keep to the script, means we're not in the flow of the energy, which makes us sound artificial or contrived. We have an agenda to deliver our lines – lines which are no longer appropriate.

Saying "yes" to things we wouldn't normally do shakes us up a little and allows us to practice being in new energy – the unfamiliar energy beyond our comfort zone. You can't learn this in a book, it takes practice.

When we become better conductors of the energy, we shine more brightly.

And when we shine brightly, we can dispel the dark night of depression.

THIRTY FOUR

Conclusion

Things are different, now that I'm on the other side of the black hole. I'm happy, but not in an adrenaline fuelled way. I'm peaceful, but not because things are quiet – the peace is bubbling with possibility. I'm free, because I've swopped the counterfeit freedom of the rebel for real freedom. It feels like I'm being driven by a different kind of force. And maybe that's the crux of the whole thing.

Physicists keep re-writing the text book when it comes to energy. First Newton discovered the force of gravity. Then came our understanding of electromagnetism, which is stronger than gravity. Now there's something called dark energy – nobody has a clue what this is, they just know there's an awful lot of it... in fact it makes up 73% of the universe.

To say that energy has no effect on us is like saying gravity doesn't apply to us, which would be ridiculous.

This just serves as a reminder – there's no need to fret about the fact that we don't understand depression. There's a lot of stuff we don't understand. The universe is mostly made up of empty space, except that it isn't empty – there's all sorts of stuff going on in what appears to be empty space.

Depression isn't a problem to fix, it's an energy we learn to understand and develop mastery over. This requires a curious (non judgmental) mind and a heart that can process emotion in present time. With these two on board, we can navigate our "inner space."

Mastery is a funny word, because it implies having complete control over something – but without being controlling. The analogy I like to use is that of being an actor. An actor can learn their lines and be technically proficient at their craft. But there's another kind of acting, in which an actor knows their craft so well that they can "forget" themselves and step into the space between actor and audience. All the magic happens in this space. It's a space of infinite possibility and huge amounts of energy. If they step into it, they can pull the audience into the space with them.

The drawback is fear. If they leave their mind behind to enter the space, they might forget the lines. They might forget how to respond to the cues of the other actors. There's a good chance they will be humiliated... on the other hand, they could be part of an experience that is transcendent, both for themselves and the audience.

It's all about the energy and the space. If we use the tools, we can become more skilled at containing the energy and navigating the space. In this way we gain freedom from destructive thoughts and emotions. If we can't manage thought, it becomes automatic and if we can't manage emotions, they become compulsive. Automatic and compulsive turn us into little more than robots, so it's no wonder we become susceptible to depression.

There is no end goal to life, just the constant expansion as the mind becomes more free and the heart becomes more loving. Never complete. Never finished. Always becoming. Always reaching for the joy.

Finally, a word about rebellion!

Rebelliousness, if it is directed against corporations and the status quo is a good thing, because it prevents us from being manipulated. When I become seduced by the amazing smell of warm croissants in the supermarket now, I imagine Donald Trump behind the counter or the bankers who screwed up, foreclosed on poor people, then paid themselves millions of dollars in bonuses. This gives me pause before handing over my money. Anger trumps self denial. It makes it easier to say no to the things corporations sell. I extend this to whatever I'm about to buy. I stop and think "do I really need this?" I walk past Starbucks these days to one of the independent coffee merchants. They need our support. Corporations don't.

So yes, rebelliousness is good if it's channelled in the right direction. However, unchecked, it can become a cynical identity that works against our liberation. I am guilty of this. I used to be extremely cynical about both traditional, and new age methods of healing, but this is throwing the good out with the bad. There are amazing, dedicated people who are full of integrity in both worlds... just as there's also blatant profiteering in both worlds.

Traditionally the way we have ascribed value to things is through money. Expensive products used high priced materials and better manufacturing processes. Once we stopped manufacturing things and became providers of services, we kept the same value system – i.e. expensive is better (even though there are no raw materials, just the energy of the personnel, which is intangible). Business consultants pick random figures out of the air, on the basis that if they go too cheap, people won't think they're any good. This philosophy has spread to the healing professions. "I'll charge more so people will think I'm better than the competition."

We need discernment.

99% of all healing comes from our commitment – what we put in. If paying thousands of dollars means we take a program more seriously, then it will be effective – not because the program is so good, but because we're taking it seriously. If we believe St Joseph's fingernail will heal us, it will, not because of the magical properties of the fingernail but because of our relationship to it.

Everything happens in the space between... in the relationship, between things.

Don't fall into the trap that you are in constant need of external resources, because if you go down this route and your life doesn't change, you can feel resentful. Workshops and seminars are great at taking you up to the penthouse and, for a fee, showing you the view. But they don't allow you to stay there. On Monday morning you're back at ground level, unless you learn to build your own scaffold.

Don't be too cynical about energy medicine, as I was. Crystals, sound, light, chakra balancing, all work – but not on a low frequency system. They work at high frequency levels. If your body is full of junk food and your mind full of junk thoughts, they have no ability to heal because they can't penetrate this density. Either you have to do some work first, or opt for the chemical medicine.

Don't be judgmental about chemical medicine, as I was. It can be invaluable, particularly at the beginning. You wouldn't be judgmental with a child who has training wheels on her bike. You are that child. And you are also the bully who is tormenting her. Learn to be more kind. Kindness is a very under rated value.

Luckily, one of the outcomes of developing the four pillars is enhanced intuition. With intuition you will be able to evaluate what's best for you, instead of blindly following the crowd. You'll know when, where, and how to seek help when it's necessary.

Don't give your authority over to an "expert". You know more than you think you know. We all have the power to tap into the source of consciousness. Therapy is great if you have spare cash. But a lot of people these days are struggling to pay a mortgage, and we need to find a way to help them. There are thousands of people suffering in silence from problems that any one of us could help with.

We need to build community.

There is an epidemic of depression. During my research I heard stories of people with depression and people with severe eating disorders who had been on waiting lists for months. When they are finally seen, what magical formula will they be given? There isn't one, apart from the obvious... loving support; encouragement to find something to love more than the condition; encouragement to give up the need to control life. Love cures things, and you don't need a diploma in how to love. You don't need a degree in how to listen.

Before my depression, a couple of high profile people committed suicide. The media covered both deaths. The response was shock and upset. Why hadn't they flagged up how they were feeling?

I decided to put this "flagging up" thing to the test over a period of a few days. When I met people and they asked how I was, instead of saying "fine" I told them I was feeling really depressed. I have to report that most people change the subject, or walk away. Maybe they're not aware that they do it. Maybe it triggers something in them. Maybe they don't know what to say.

If it's the latter, just say something like "d'you want to talk about it?" They might say yes, they'll probably say no, but they'll appreciate you asking. And they'll feel relief that they were able to be honest. The walking away just reinforces the stigma. It encourages pretending and inauthenticity.

We all have to live with the possibility of depression, because we live in a world of duality. We contain the potential for good and bad; light and dark; greedy and generous; honest and fraudulent; hero and coward; cool and boring; masculine and feminine. Life is not a journey up a ladder of success, it's a tightrope walk, a balancing act.

We find centre. We're never in the centre for very long. But that's ok, as long as we learn to love the high wire.

I used to think the word *balance* was boring. Now I realise it's one of the most exciting things in the world.

It's those, rubbish inadequate words again... what can you do?

When I sat in the park today, I watched a man walking his dog. The dog suddenly ran towards the pond and jumped in, splashing about playfully. The dog's obvious joy made me laugh, but the man was FURIOUS. He shouted and screamed and when the dog finally emerged sheepishly, he beat it to "teach it a lesson". The dog was just being a dog. It was the man who had a problem – he couldn't contain the feeling of not being able to control things. It was a sad tableau, but what's more sad is that we do this to ourselves. We beat ourselves mercilessly for our imagined indiscretions.

My biggest breakthrough came when I stopped trying to control my mind and started to love it instead. As a consequence, I became kinder – to me and to other people. I didn't have to pretend anymore. When I stopped pretending I had more energy. I was happy, because I felt more real.

It makes sense really. Love is the only thing that heals. It heals unruly children and it heals the childish parts of our own nature – the jealous, greedy, angry, humiliated parts. That way, they grow up so we don't have to spend so much time controlling them. We can live a more spontaneous life without the fear that they'll show up and embarrass us.

The Beatles were right. All you need is love. Not "real world" love, the kind with all the conditions attached. That love is ineffective. When we love something in the real world, we *lose* power, because "it" has power over us. That's why it can so easily be turned into an addiction. When we move into the energy world and love from there, we *gain* power. We can love without the impulse to leave ourselves. This love can heal the world.

Einstein, no stranger to the fifth dimension, knew a secret he only revealed to his friends and relatives. He said that the energy of the universe was love, but that people weren't ready to hear that... just yet.

Perhaps we're ready now.

My boyfriend didn't come back. But I'm more comfortable with the space between us. When I lean into it, the pain has gone. There's no loss or regret. The space makes me smile.

I never got my Meet Cute, but in the process of the depression, I met myself. And far from the horrid creature of my darkest imaginings, I found out, I was actually pretty cute myself.

Lightning Source UK Ltd.
Milton Keynes UK
UKOW06f0918291215

265472UK00018B/842/P